CADOGAN CHESS BOOKS

The Modern
French Tarrasch

CADOGAN CHESS BOOKS

Chief Advisor: Garry Kasparov
Editor: Andrew Kinsman
Russian Series Editor: Ken Neat

Other titles in this series include:

BAGIROV, V.
English Opening: Classical & Indian
English Opening: Symmetrical

BASMAN, M.
The Killer Grob
The New St. George

DONALDSON, J. & SILMAN, J.
Accelerated Dragons

GLIGORIC, S.
The Nimzo-Indian Defence

GUFELD, E.
An Opening Repertoire for the
   Attacking Player

KRASENKOV, M.
The Open Spanish
The Sveshnikov Sicilian

NORWOOD, D.
The Modern Benoni

SOKOLOV, I.
Nimzo-Indian Defence:
   Classical Variation

TAULBUT, S.
The New Bogo-Indian

WATSON, J.
Play the French
   (New Edition)

For a complete catalogue of CADOGAN CHESS books (which includes the former Pergamon Chess and Maxwell Macmillan Chess list) please write to:

Cadogan Books, London House, Parkgate Road, London SW11 4NQ
Tel: (0171) 738 1961
Fax: (0171) 924 5491

The Modern French Tarrasch

by

Eduard Gufeld

Translated and Edited by Ken Neat

CADOGAN
chess
LONDON, NEW YORK

English Translation Copyright © 1996 Ken Neat

First published 1996 by Cadogan Books plc, London House, Parkgate Road, London SW11 4NQ.

Distributed in North America by Simon and Schuster, Paramount Publishing, 200 Old Tappan Road, Old Tappan, New Jersey 07675, USA.

British Library Cataloguing in Publication Data
A CIP catalogue record for this book is available from the British Library

ISBN 1 85744 103 6

Typeset by Ken Neat, Durham

Printed in Great Britain by BPC Wheatons Ltd, Exeter

Contents

Conventional Signs

!	good move
!!	excellent move
!?	move deserving consideration
?!	dubious move
?	incorrect move
??	blunder
±±	decisive advantage for White
∓∓	decisive advantage for Black
±	clear advantage for White
∓	clear advantage for Black
⩲	slight advantage for White
⩱	slight advantage for Black
∞	unclear position
⯢	with compensation for the material
→	with an attack
↑	with the initiative
Δ	with the idea of
Ch	Championship
corr.	correspondence game

Introduction

In the Tarrasch Variation of the French Defence **1 e4 e6 2 d4 d5 3 ♘d2 c5**, the **4 exd5** line has undergone a genuine re-evaluation in the last decade. The following question is now close to being resolved – is Black obliged to play the position leading to an isolated pawn after 4...exd5, which in the recent past was considered obligatory, or can he avoid this? Indeed, the slow, tedious struggle for a draw, with piece manoeuvring around the isolated d5 pawn, is not to everyone's taste. A different situation arises after **4...♕xd5**. Let us take a look at the resulting position.

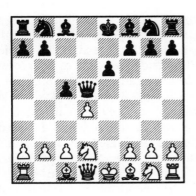

Black's pawn formation has the undoubted virtue of containing no weaknesses. The only question is – can he risk conceding several tempi with the temporary deferment of his development, for the sake of avoiding positions with the potential drawbacks inherent in an isolated pawn? The extensive experience of the past decade has given a positive reply. Black succeeds in successfully completing his development, with good prospects of active counterplay. It is not without reason that in recent times, in order to deprive Black of this possibility, White has often switched to **4 ♘gf3**, in order after the exchange on d5 to avoid the capture with the queen. However, apart from the fact that this reduces White's potential possibilities in positions arising after 5 exd5 exd5, Black can also avoid capturing with the pawn and can implement the concept of active piece play. This monograph has the aim of examining the possibilities for both sides, arising in the event of Black avoiding positions with an isolated d5 pawn, and consists of three main sections:

4 ♘gf3 and rare 4th moves for White (Chapters 1-3);

4 exd5 ♕xd5 – deviations from the main line (Chapters 4-9);

The main line – **4 exd5 ♕xd5 5 ♘gf3 cxd4 6 ♗c4 ♕d6 7 0-0 ♘f6 8 ♘b3 ♘c6 9 ♘bxd4 ♘xd4 10 ♘xd4** (Chapters 10-19).

1   Rare Lines: 4 dxc5 and 4 c3

1	e4	e6
2	d4	d5
3	♘d2	c5

In this chapter we will examine the rare continuations **4 dxc5 (1.1)** and **4 c3 (1.2)**.

4 ♗b5+ has no independent significance, since after 4...♘c6 5 exd5 ♕xd5! 6 ♘gf3 cxd4 play transposes into set-ups considered in later chapters. For example: 7 ♗c4 ♕d6 8 0–0 ♗e7 (8...♘f6 is also good, with an extra tempo compared with the main line) 9 ♘e4 ♕b4 10 ♕d3 ♘f6 11 a3 ♕b6 12 b4 a6 13 ♗b2 0–0 14 ♖fe1 ♘xe4 15 ♖xe4 ♗f6 16 ♖d1 e5∓ (Valenti-Huss, Lugano 1989).

Also possible is 4...♗d7 5 ♗xd7+ ♕xd7 6 exd5 ♕xd5! 7 ♕f3 ♘f6 8 ♘e2 ♘c6 9 dxc5 ♕xf3 10 ♘xf3 ♗xc5 11 0–0 ♔e7= (Kagan-Moutousis, Greek Ch 1994).

1.1

(1 e4 e6 2 d4 d5 3 ♘d2 c5)

4	dxc5	♗xc5

Weaker is 4...♘f6 5 exd5 ♕xd5 6 ♘b3 ♕xd1+ 7 ♔xd1 ♘a6 8 ♗xa6 bxa6 9 ♘f3 ♗b7 10 ♔e2 ♖c8 11 c4 ♗xc5 12 ♘xc5 ♖xc5 13 b3± (Bronstein-Ab.Khasin, Kislovodsk 1969).

5	♗d3

After 5 ♘b3 ♗b6 6 exd5, apart from 6...exd5, where Black has an extra tempo compared with the main variation 4 exd5 exd5 (which falls outside the scope of the present book), he can also play 6...♘f6! 7 ♗b5+ ♗d7 8 ♗xd7+ ♕xd7 9 c4 exd5 10 c5 ♗c7 11 ♘f3 ♘c6 12 0–0 0–0 13 ♘bd4 ♘xd4 14 ♕xd4 ♖fe8 15 ♗e3 ♖e4 16 ♕d3 ♖ae8∓ (Steinitz-Lasker, Nürnberg 1896).

5	...	♘f6

Also good is 5...♘c6 6 exd5 ♕xd5 (6...exd5 7 ♘b3 ♗b6 8 ♘f3 ♘ge7 9 0–0 0–0 10 c3 ♕d6 11 ♖e1 ♘g6 12 ♗e3 ♗xe3 13 ♖xe3±, Spielmann-Alekhine, New York 1927) 7 ♕g4 (7 ♘e4 ♗b6 8 c4 ♕d8!=) 7...♘e5! 8 ♕xg7 ♗d4 9

♕g3 ♘f6, and the initiative is with Black, who has a flexible pawn structure in the centre with the possibility of ...e6-e5 (Alekhine).

6 e5

6 ♕e2 0–0 7 ♘gf3 ♘c6 8 e5 ♘g4 9 0–0 f6 10 ♘b3 ♗xf2+ 11 ♖xf2 ♘xf2 12 ♕xf2 fxe5 13 ♗xh7+ ♚xh7 14 ♘g5+ ♚g8 15 ♕h4 ♕b6+ 16 ♗e3 ♕xe3+ 17 ♚h1 ♖f5 18 ♕h7+ ♚f8∓ (Landenbergue-Huss, Swiss Ch 1993).

6 ... ♘fd7
7 ♘gf3 ♘c6
8 ♕e2 ♕c7

8...f6! 9 exf6 ♕xf6 10 ♘b3 h6 11 ♘xc5 ♘xc5∓ (Alekhine).

9 ♘b3 ♗b6!

9...♗e7?! 10 ♗f4 f6 11 ♗b5 ♘dxe5 12 ♘xe5 fxe5 13 ♗xe5 ♗d6 14 f4!± (Spielmann-Asztalos, Bled 1931).

10 ♗f4 f6! 11 ♗b5 0–0∓.

1.2

(1 e4 e6 2 d4 d5 3 ♘d2 c5)

4 c3 cxd4
4...♘c6:

(a) 5 exd5 ♕xd5 6 dxc5 ♗xc5 7 ♘gf3 ♘f6 8 ♗c4 ♕h5 9 0–0 0–0 10 ♕c2 ♗d7 11 ♘e4 ♘xe4 12 ♕xe4 ♖ae8 13 ♖d1 ♗c8 14 ♗e3 f5 15 ♕f4 ♗xe3 16 ♕xe3 f4 17 ♕e4 ♚h8 18 ♖e1 e5∓ (Bodor-Holzke, Budapest 1990);

(b) 5 ♘gf3 ♘f6 6 ♗d3 cxd4 7 cxd4 ♕b6 8 e5 ♘d7 9 ♘b3 ♗b4+ 10 ♗d2 a5 11 ♗xb4 ♕xb4+ 12

♕d2 a4 13 ♘c1 ♘b6 14 ♘e2 ♗d7 15 ♖c1 ♕xd2+ 16 ♚xd2 ♚e7 17 ♘c3 ♖hc8= (Katalymov-Lputian, Daugavpils 1978).

5 cxd4

5 ... ♘c6

5...dxe4 6 ♘xe4 ♘f6 7 ♘xf6+ ♕xf6 8 ♘f3 ♗b4+ 9 ♗d2 ♗xd2+ 10 ♕xd2 ♗d7 11 ♘e5 ♗c6 12 ♖c1 0–0 13 ♗d3 ♗d5= (Crawley-Hübner, Lugano 1989).

6 ♘gf3 dxe4

6...♕b6 7 ♕a4?! ♗d7 8 ♗b5? (8 exd5) 8...dxe4 9 ♘xe4 a6∓ (Süchting-Alekhine, Karlsbad 1911).

7 ♘xe4 ♗e7

7...♗b4+ 8 ♗d2 ♗xd2+ 9 ♕xd2 ♘f6 10 ♗d3 0–0 11 ♖c1 ♕e7 12 0–0 ♖d8 13 ♘xf6+ ♕xf6 14 ♖fd1 ♗d7 15 ♗e4 ♗e8 16 ♕d3± (Crawley-Levitt, British Ch 1987).

8 ♗d3 ♘f6
9 0–0 0–0

10 ♗e3 ♘b4 11 ♘xf6+ ♗xf6 12 ♗e4 ♘d5 13 ♖c1 b6= (Milner-Barry–Lilienthal, Hastings 1934/5).

2   4 ♘gf3 ♘f6

1	e4	e6
2	d4	d5
3	♘d2	c5
4	♘gf3	

The inclusion of 4 ♘gf3 is employed in order to make the capture 5 exd5 one move later and avoid the recapture 5...♕xd5, if Black should aim for this by transposition of moves (for example, by 4...♘f6 5 exd5 ♕xd5). However, apart from the fact that this move order reduces White's potential possibilities in positions with an isolated pawn (after 5...exd5), even after this continuation Black can avoid capturing with the pawn and can implement the concept of active piece play.

Since this monograph has the aim of examining the methods of play for Black, arising in the event of him avoiding positions with an isolated d5 pawn, we will not consider the variation 4...a6 5 exd5 exd5. We will fully examine the variation **4...cxd4** (Chapter 3), but in the present chapter after 4...♘f6 5 exd5 we will restrict ourselves only to the move 5...♘xd5.

4	...	♘f6

A logical reply, if Black is aiming for the type of game examined in later chapters of the book.

Unless Black is willing to play positions with an isolated d-pawn, he should avoid 4...♘c6, since after

5 exd5 his only feasible reply is 5...exd5. Instead 5...♘xd4? can be met by 6 ♘xd4 cxd4 7 ♗b5+ ♗d7 8 dxe6± (Aronin-Batuev, USSR 1949), and 5...♕xd5 allows White a pleasant choice:

(a) 6 ♗c4 ♕d8 (6...♕d6? 7 ♘e4) 7 dxc5 (or 7 ♘b3 cxd4 8 0-0, transposing into positions from Chapter 6) 7...♗xc5 8 ♕e2 ♕c7 9 ♘e4 ♗e7 10 0-0 ♘f6 11 ♖d1 0-0 12 ♗g5± (Aronin-Matsukevich, USSR 1961);

(b) 6 c4 ♕h5 7 d5! exd5 8 cxd5 ♕xd5 9 ♗c4±.

Note that the position often reached via 4...♘c6 5 ♗b5 cxd4 6 ♘xd4 is covered in Chapter 3 under the move order 4...cxd4 5 ♘xd4 ♘c6 6 ♗b5.

Now the most popular replies are **5 exd5 (2.1)** and **5 ♗b5+ (2.2)**.

5 e5 ♘fd7 leads to a double-edged position which usually arises from the move order 3...♘f6 4 e5 ♘fd7 5 ♘gf3 (ECO index C05) and is outside the scope of this book.

2.1

(1 e4 e6 2 d4 d5 3 ♘d2 c5 4 ♘gf3 ♘f6)

5 exd5

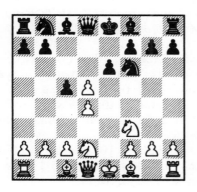

White is aiming for positions with an isolated pawn, although it has to be said that his possibilities here are reduced in comparison with 4 exd5. However, Black is by no means obliged to go in for this.

5 ... ♘xd5

Evidently the best reply if Black wants to avoid 5...exd5, since after the thematic 5...♕xd5 6 ♗c4 White can answer 6...♕d6 with 7 dxc5 ♕xc5, and if 6...♕d8 he can again transpose by 7 0-0 cxd4 8 ♘b3 into the variation examined in Chapter 6.

After 6...♕c6 7 a4 a6 Black has to reckon with the sharp reply 8 ♗b5 axb5 9 axb5 ♕xf3 10 ♖xa8!, which gives White the advantage after both 10...♕xg2 11 ♕f3 ♕xf3 12 ♘xf3 ♘fd7 13 ♘e5, and 10...♕xd1+ 11 ♔xd1 ♘fd7 (or 11...♗d6 12 dxc5) 12 ♘c4 with the threats of 13 ♗f4 and 13 ♘e5.

Keres also recommended the more modest 8 0-0 b6 9 ♘e5 ♕c7 10 ♖e1 ♘c6 11 ♘df3 ♘xe5 12 dxe5 ♘d7 13 ♕e2 ♗b7 14 ♗g5±, or 8 ♕e2 b6 9 ♘b3 ♗b7 10 dxc5 ♗xc5 11 ♘xc5 bxc5 12 0-0±.

6 ♘b3

The fashionable continuation, although 6 ♘e4 is still topical:

(a) 6...cxd4 7 ♘xd4 ♗e7 8 ♗e2 0-0 9 0-0 e5 10 ♘b5 ♘c6= (Keres-Bronstein, USSR Ch 1947);

(b) 6...♘d7 7 a3 ♘5f6 8 ♘xf6+ ♘xf6 9 ♗d3 cxd4 10 0-0 ♗e7 11 ♘xd4 0-0 12 ♖e1 ♗d7 13 ♕e2 ♕b6 14 ♘f3 ♖fd8= (Gufeld-Korchnoi, USSR 1972) – *Game 1*.

Now Black's main replies are **6...cxd4 (2.11)** and **6...♘d7 (2.12)**.

2.11

(1 e4 e6 2 d4 d5 3 ♘d2 c5 4 ♘gf3 ♘f6 5 exd5 ♘xd5 6 ♘b3)

6 ... cxd4
7 ♘bxd4

This position can also be reached via the move order 1 e4 e6 2 d4 d5 3 ♘d2 c5 4 ♘gf3 cxd4 5 ♘xd4 ♘f6 6 exd5 ♘xd5 7 ♘2f3.

7 ...   ♗e7

(a) 7...♗b4+ 8 ♗d2 ♗xd2+ 9 ♕xd2 0-0 10 ♗c4 b6 11 0-0-0 ♗b7 12 ♖he1 ♕c8 13 ♗xd5 ♗xd5 14 ♘f5 exf5 15 ♕xd5 ♘c6 16 ♘e5± (Kengis-Glek, Bad Godesburg 1993);

(b) 7...a6 8 c3 ♕c7 9 ♗d3 ♗f4 10 ♗xf4 ♕xf4 11 ♕e2 ♗e7 12 0-0 0-0= (T.Horvath-Glek, Bundesliga 1995).

8   ♗d3

(a) 8 ♗c4 0-0 9 0-0 ♘c6 10 c3 ♗f6 11 ♖e1 ♗ce7 12 ♗g5 ♕c7= (Eingorn-Nogueiras, Havana 1986);

(b) 8 ♗e2 a6! (8...0-0 9 0-0 a6 10 c4 ♘b4 11 ♗e3 ♕c7 12 a3 ♘4c6 13 ♕c2 ♘xd4 14 ♘xd4 ♗d7 15 b4 ♘c6 16 ♘b3±, Savon-Petrosian, USSR Ch 1973) 9 c4 ♘f6 10 0-0 ♕c7 11 ♖e1?! (11 ♕c2!? △ 11...e5?! 12 ♘f5) 11...e5! 12 ♘c2 0-0 13 ♗g5 ♖d8 14 ♕c1 ♘c6∓ (Eingorn-Dreev, Lucerne 1993) – *Game 2*;

(c) 8 g3 0-0 9 ♗g2 b5 (9...♗d7 10 0-0 ♘c6 11 ♘xc6 ♗xc6 12 ♘e5±, Jansa-Korchnoi, Nice Olympiad 1974; 9...♗f6 10 0-0 ♘e7 11 ♗g5±) 10 0-0 a6 11 ♕e2 ♗f6 12 ♖d1 ♕b6 13 a4 b4 14 a5 ♕c5= (Kengis-Gulko, Riga 1995).

8 ...   0-0

8...♘d7 9 0-0 ♘c5 10 ♗b5+ ♗d7 11 ♗xd7+ ♕xd7 12 c4 ♘b4 13 ♘e5±.

9   0-0

9 c3 ♘d7 10 0-0 ♖e8 11 ♖e1 ♗f6 12 ♗c2 a6 13 ♕d3 g6 14 ♗h6 ♕c7 15 ♖ad1 ♘7b6 16 ♗b3± (Yakovich-Budnikov, St Petersburg 1993).

9 ...   ♘d7

(a) 9...♗f6?! 10 c4 (10 ♖e1 ♘b4 11 ♗e4± (King-Dolmatov, Reykjavik 1990) 10...♘b4 11 ♗e4 ♕e7 12 a3 ♘4c6 13 ♘xc6 ♘xc6 14 ♕c2 g6 15 ♗e3± (A.Ivanov-Gulko, USA Ch 1995);

(b) 9...b6!? 10 ♗e4 ♗b7 11 c4 ♘c3 12 ♗xh7+ ♔xh7 13 bxc3 ♘d7∞ (Yermolinsky);

(c) 9...♘c6!? (Orlov).

10   c4   ♘5f6

10...♘b4 11 ♗b1 ♗f6 12 ♕e2 ♘b6 13 ♖d1 ♕c7 14 b3 ♗d7 15 a3 ♘a6 16 ♖a2± (Buljovic-Planinc, Novi Sad 1965).

11   ♗f4   ♘h5
12   ♗e3   g6?!

12...♘hf6 △ ...♕c7±.

13   ♖e1   a6
14   ♖c1   ♖e8
15   ♗f1   ♗f8

16 a3 b6 17 b4 ♗b7 18 ♘b3 ♘hf6 19 ♗d4 a5 20 c5± Spasov-Dreev (Moscow Olympiad 1994).

2.12

(1 e4 e6 2 d4 d5 3 ♘d2 c5 4 ♘gf3 ♘f6 5 exd5 ♘xd5 6 ♘b3)

6 ...   ♘d7
7 c4

(a) 7 ♗c4 ♘7b6 8 ♗e2 c4 9 ♘c5 ♕c7 10 ♘e4 c3 (Smagin-Lputian, Yugoslavia 1991 – *Game 3*) 11 0-0∞;

(b) 7 ♗g5 ♗e7 8 ♗xe7 ♕xe7 9 ♗b5 cxd4 10 ♕xd4 0-0 11 0-0-0 a6 12 ♗c4 ♘5f6 13 ♖he1 b5 14 ♗d5! ♘xd5 15 ♕xd5 ♖a7 16 ♕d6 ♕xd6 17 ♖xd6± (Popovic-Nikolic, Yugoslavia 1991);

(c) 7 g3 cxd4?! (7...♗e7!?) 8 ♗g2 ♗b4+ 9 ♗d2 e5 (9...d3 10 c4!) 10 0-0 0-0 11 ♖e1 f6 12 ♘fxd4 ♘7b6 13 ♗xb4 ♘xb4 14 ♕d2 ♘4d5 15 ♘b5!± (Svidler-Belyavsky, Yugoslavia 1995).

7 ...   ♘5f6
8 ♗e2

8 dxc5 ♕c7! (8...♘xc5!? 9 ♕xd8+ ♔xd8 10 ♘e5 ♘xb3 11 axb3 ♗b4+ 12 ♗d2 ♗xd2+ 13 ♔xd2 ♔e7=, E.Vladimirov) 9 ♗d3 (9 g3 ♘xc5 10 ♗g2 ♘xb3 11 ♕xb3 ♗d6 12 0-0 0-0 13 ♖d1 e5 14 ♗g5 ♘e4 15 ♕d3 f5∞, Belyavsky-Nikolic, Barcelona 1989 – *Game 4*) 9...♘xc5 10 ♘xc5 ♗xc5 11 0-0 ♗d7 (11...b6 12 b4!±) 12 ♕e2 ♗c6 13 ♘e5 ♖d8! 14 ♗f4 ♖d4= (Kotronias-E.Vladimirov, Moscow 1989).

8 ...   ♗e7
9 0-0

9 dxc5 0-0 10 0-0 ♕c7 11 ♘fd4 ♘xc5?! (11...a6!?∞) 12 ♘b5 ♕b6 13 ♗f4 ♗d7 14 ♗c7 ♕a6 15 ♗d6 ♗xd6 16 ♘xd6 ♘xb3 17 axb3± (Rohde-Lputian, Los Angeles 1991).

9 ...   b6
10 ♗f4   ♗b7
11 ♘e5   0-0

11...♘xe5 12 ♗xe5 ♘d7 13 ♗f3 ♗xf3 14 ♕xf3 0-0 15 ♗g3 ♕c8 16 ♖ad1 a5 17 d5 exd5 18 ♖xd5± (Vasyukov-Lputian, Yerevan 1994).

12 ♗f3   ♕c8
13 ♖c1   ♖d8
14 ♕e2   ♘xe5
15 ♗xe5   ♗xf3
16 ♕xf3   ♘d7

17 ♗g3 ½-½ (Arnason-Gulko, Groningen 1990).

2.2

(1 e4 e6 2 d4 d5 3 ♘d2 c5 4 ♘gf3 ♘f6)

5 ♗b5+

The modern method of playing this variation, which has yet to demonstrate its superiority over the classical 5 exd5.

>   5   ...   &d7
>   6   &xd7+   ♘bxd7

6...♕xd7 7 exd5 ♕xd5 8 c4 ♕d8 9 ♘b3 cxd4 10 ♘bxd4 &b4+ 11 &d2 ♕a5 12 a3 &xd2+ 13 ♕xd2 ♕xd2+ 14 ♔xd2 ♘bd7= (Timman-Bareev, Wijk aan Zee 1995).

>   7   e5   ♘e4
>   8   ♘xe4   dxe4
>   9   ♘g5   cxd4
>   10   ♕xd4   ♕a5+
>   11   &d2   ♕xe5
>   12   ♕xe5   ♘xe5
>   13   &c3

13 ♘xe4 ♘c6 14 0-0-0 ♖d8 15 &e3 &e7 16 ♖xd8+ ♔xd8 17 ♖d1+ ♔c7= (Van der Wiel-Bareev, Wijk aan Zee 1995).

13...♘c6 14 0-0-0 e3 15 fxe3 &e7 16 ♘f3 f6 17 ♘d4 ♘xd4 18 ♖xd4 &c5= (Van der Wiel-Bareev, Wijk aan Zee 1995).

Game 1
Gufeld–Korchnoi
USSR 1972

>   1   e4   e6
>   2   d4   d5
>   3   ♘d2   c5
>   4   ♘gf3   ♘f6
>   5   exd5   ♘xd5
>   6   ♘e4   ♘d7
>   7   a3!?   ♘5f6
>   8   ♘xf6+   ♘xf6
>   9   &d3   cxd4
>   10   0-0   &e7

In the event of 10...&c5 11 b4! (this is the idea of 7 a3) 11...&b6 12 &b2 White regains his pawn with an appreciable advantage.

>   11   ♘xd4   0-0
>   12   ♖e1   &d7
>   13   ♕e2   ♕b6
>   14   ♘f3   ♖fd8
>   15   c4   a5
>   16   &g5   h6
>   17   &h4   &a4?!

This bishop should have been kept close to the king.

>   18   ♖ac1   ♔f8
>   19   ♖c3   ♖ac8
>   20   &b1   &b3?!

It was not yet too late for 20...&e8.

>   21   ♘e5!   a4
>   22   ♖e3   ♕d4?
>   23   ♘xf7!   ♕xh4

The best chance. 23...♔xf7 would have lost quickly to 24 ♖xb3! axb3 25 ♕xe6+ ♔f8 26 &g6! ♕xc4 27 ♕xe7+ ♔g8 28 &xf6.

24 ᐁe5!   ᑲxc4!
25 ᐁg6+   ᑭf7
26 ᐁxh4?

White could have won by 26 ᑭxe6! ᑲxe2 27 ᑭxe7+ ᑭg8 28 ᐁxh4.

26 ...   ᑲxe2
27 ᑭ3xe2   ᐁd7!
28 ᐁf3?

This finally loses White his advantage, which he could still have retained by 28 ᐁf5! ᐁc5 29 ᐁxe7 ᑭxe7 30 ᑭc1, planning the manoeuvre ᑭc4-b4.

28 ...   ᐁc5
29 h4   ᑲf6
30 g4?!   ᐁd3!
31 ᑲxd3   ᑭxd3
32 ᑭg2   ᑭc4
33 ᑭe4   ᑭxe4
34 ᑭxe4   b5
35 ᐁe5+!

Black's bishop is too dangerous.

35 ...   ᑲxe5

36 ᑭxe5 ᑭb3 37 ᑭe2 ᑭf6 38 f3 g5 39 h5! ᑭf7 40 ᑭg3 ᑭe7 41

ᑭd2! e5 42 ᑭf2 ᑭe6 43 ᑭg2 e4! 44 fxe4 ᑭe5 45 ᑭe2 ᑭd3 46 ᑭf2 ᑭd4 47 ᑭf3 b4 48 axb4 ᑭxb4 49 ᑭg3! ᑭxe4 50 ᑭf2 ᑭb4 51 ᑭf5+ ᑭd4 52 ᑭf6 ᑭb3+ 53 ᑭg2 ᑭxb2+ 54 ᑭg3 ᑭb3+ 55 ᑭg2 a3 56 ᑭxh6 ᑭc3 57 ᑭa6 **draw agreed**

Game 2
Eingorn–Dreev
Lucerne 1993

---

1   e4   e6
2   d4   d5
3   ᐁd2   c5
4   ᐁgf3   cxd4
5   ᐁxd4   ᐁf6
6   exd5   ᐁxd5
7   ᐁ2f3   ᑲe7
8   ᑲe2

8 ᑲd3 is considered the main continuation.

8   ...   a6!

Preparing a good post for the queen at c7.

9   c4   ᐁf6
10   0-0

White cannot prevent ...ᕻc7 (10 ᑲf4 ᕻa5+ 11 ᑲd2 ᕻc7).

10   ...   ᕻc7
11   ᑭe1?!

Black is obviously planning ...e6-e5, and so it made sense to find a more active post for the knight. 11 ᕻc2 0-0 (11...e5?! 12 ᐁf5) 12 ᑲg5 was therefore more logical.

11   ...   e5
12   ᐁc2   0-0
13   ᑲg5   ᑭd8
14   ᕻc1   ᐁc6

15 ♘d2

The immediate 15 ♘e3 was perhaps more logical, although after 15...♗e6 16 ♖d1 Black's chances are nevertheless preferable.

15 ...   ♗f5!
16 ♘e3?!

But now he should have 'changed tune' and played 16 ♗f3!, with the intention of exchanging the knight at c6.

16 ...   ♗e6
17 ♗xf6   ♗xf6
18 ♘e4   ♗e7
19 c5

If 19 ♘c3 there would have followed 19...♗g5, but perhaps White should have agreed to this, since now the c5 pawn is weak and Black finds another way of activating his dark-square bishop.

19 ...   ♖d4!
20 ♘d2?!

20 ♘g3 was a tougher defence, aiming for f5, although after 20...g6 the threat of ...f7-f5 leaves him poorly placed. But now his game quickly goes downhill.

20	...	♗xc5!
21	♘f3	♗b4
22	♖f1	♖d7
23	♗c4	♗xc4
24	♕xc4	♖ad8
25	h4	♗d2
26	♘f5	♘d4
27	♕d3	♘c2
28	♕e4	♘xa1
29	♘xe5	♖e8

White resigns

Game 3
Smagin–Lputian
Yugoslavia 1991

1	e4	e6
2	d4	d5
3	♘d2	c5
4	♘gf3	♘f6
5	exd5	♘xd5
6	♘b3	♘d7
7	♗c4	♘7b6
8	♗e2	c4
9	♘c5	♕c7
10	♘e4	c3
11	b3?	

An unjustified concession. Now the 'wedge' at c3 cleaves White's position into two parts. 11 0-0 is more natural and stronger.

11	...	♗e7
12	0-0	0-0
13	♖e1	♗d7
14	h4	♖ad8
15	h5	♘f6
16	♗g5	

16 ♘xf6+ ♗xf6 17 h6 ♗c6 favours Black.

16 ... ♘bd5

17 ♘g3?

White unjustifiably avoids simplifying the position, although after 17 ♘xf6+ ♗xf6 18 h6 (if 18 ♗xf6 gxf6! Black acquires the g-file for the attack) 18...g6 19 ♕c1 Black's chances are still preferable.

17 ... h6
18 ♗h4 ♘g4

18...♕f4 is also good.

19 ♗xe7 ♘xe7
20 ♕d3

Here White's queen is insecurely placed. Instead he should have weakened Black's chances on the long diagonal – 20 ♗d3 ♗c6 21 ♗e4.

20 ... ♘d5
21 ♘e5?

What is this – a blunder or a pawn sacrifice? After 21 ♘g5 hxg5 22 ♗xg4 ♘f4 23 ♕e3 ♗c6 Black stands better, but White can still put up a fight.

21 ... ♘b4
22 ♕d1 ♘xe5
23 dxe5 ♗c6!

More energetic than 23...♕xe5.

24 ♕c1

24 ♗d3 is met by 24...♗b5.

24 ... ♖d2
25 ♗d3 ♖d8
26 ♗e4 ♕b6

The immediate 26...♗xe4 is simpler.

27 ♖e3 ♗xe4
28 ♘xe4 ♖xc2
29 ♕f1 ♕d4
30 ♘d6 ♖xa2
31 ♖xa2 ♘xa2
32 ♖d3 ♕f4
33 g3

Or 33 ♖f3 ♕xf3 34 gxf3 c2.

33 ... ♕c1
34 ♖d1 ♕g5
White resigns

Game 4
Belyavsky–Nikolic
Barcelona 1989

---

1 e4 e6
2 d4 d5
3 ♘d2 c5
4 ♘gf3 ♘f6
5 exd5 ♘xd5
6 ♘b3 ♘d7
7 c4 ♘5f6
8 dxc5 ♕c7
9 g3!?

White is aiming for a Catalan-type position. The 'normal' move is 9 ♗e2 or 9 ♗d3.

9 ... ♘xc5

	10	♗g2

10 ♗f4 can be met by 10...♕c6
11 ♗g2 ♕e4+ 12 ♕e2 ♘d3+.

10	...	♘xb3
11	♕xb3	♗d6

Otherwise White will gain a
tempo by ♗f4.

12	0-0	0-0
13	♖d1	e5
14	♗g5	♘e4
15	♕d3	f5
16	♕d5+	♕f7
17	♕xf7+	♔xf7

If 17...♖xf7? the exchange
sacrifice 18 ♖xd6! ♘xd6 19 ♘xe5
♖c7 20 ♖d1 gives White more than
sufficient compensation. But now
18 ♖xd6!? ♘xd6 19 ♘xe5+ can be
met by 19...♔e6 20 ♖e1 ♘e4 with
approximate equality (Nikolic).

18	♗e3	♗c7
19	♖d5	♖e8
20	♖ad1	h6
21	♖b5	♘f6
22	♘h4	a6
23	♖b3	e4

24	♗h3	g6?!

Black provokes complications
involving a pawn sacrifice, whereas
he could have tried to demonstrate
that White's manoeuvres on moves
22 and 24 were harmless: 24...g5!?
25 ♘xf5 g4 26 ♘xh6+ ♔g6 27 ♗g2
♖h8 28 c5 ♖xh6 29 ♗xh6 ♔xh6
with a complicated endgame
(Nikolic).

25	♗xh6	b5!?
26	cxb5	♗e6
27	♖c3	♗e5
28	♖c5	♘d7
29	♖c2?	

This loses White the advantage
that he could have achieved by 29
♖c6! axb5 30 ♘xg6! ♔xg6 31
♖xd7 ♖xa2 32 ♖d5! But now the
pressure of Black's pieces on the
queenside fully compensates for the
pawn.

29	...	axb5
30	b3	♗f6
31	♗e3	♘e5
32	♖c7+	♖e7
33	♖xe7+	♗xe7
34	♖c1	♖xa2
35	♖c7	♖a1+
36	♗f1	♖d1
37	♗g5	♖d7
38	♖xd7	♗xd7
39	♗xe7	♔xe7
40	♗e2	♔d6
41	f4!	

Otherwise after 41 ♔f1 ♔c5
White might even lose.

41	...	exf3
42	♘xf3	♘xf3+
43	♗xf3	♔c5

44	**♔f2**	**♗e6**

Black wins a pawn, but White succeeds in reducing to a theoretically drawn ending. Nikolic gives the more cunning continuation 44... ♔d4!? 45 ♔e2! ♗e6 (45...♔c3 46 ♗d5) 46 b4 ♔c3 47 ♗c6! ♔xb4 48 ♗e8 g5 49 h4 gxh4 50 gxh4, which also leads to a draw.

45	**♔e3**	**♗xb3**
46	**h4**	**b4**

Or 46...♗e6 47 ♔d3 ♗c4+ 48 ♔d2! b4 49 g4 f4 50 h5 etc.

47	**g4!**	**fxg4**
48	**♗xg4**	**♗f7**
49	**♔d3**	**♔d5**
50	**♗f3+**	**♔e5**
51	**♗e4**	**b3**
52	**♗c6**	**♔f4**
53	**♔c3**	**♔g4**
54	**♗e4**	**♔h5**
55	**♗d3**	**♗e6**
56	**♗e4**	**♗f5**
57	**♗d5**	**♔xh4**
58	**♗xb3**	**♔g3**
59	**♔d2**	**♔f2**
60	**♗f7**	
	draw agreed	

3   4 ♘gf3 cxd4

1	e4	e6
2	d4	d5
3	♘d2	c5
4	♘gf3	cxd4

A fashionable continuation, based on the possibility of transposing into the Modern French Tarrasch after 5 exd5 ♕xd5.

5 ♘xd4

The natural reply, although the pawn sacrifice 5 e5 ♘c6 6 ♘b3 is also encountered:

(a) 6...♗b4+ 7 ♗d2 ♕b6 8 ♗xb4 ♕xb4+ 9 ♕d2 ♕xd2+ 10 ♔xd2± (Ermenkov-Cosma, Budapest Zonal 1993);

(b) 6...♕c7 7 ♘bxd4 ♘xe5 8 ♘b5 ♕b8 9 ♗f4 ♘d3+ 10 ♕xd3 ♕xf4 11 g3 ♕b4+ 12 c3 ♕a5 13 ♗g2 a6 14 ♘bd4 ♘f6 15 0-0 ♗d6 16 ♖fe1 0-0 17 ♘e5∞ (Rayner-Levitt, British Ch 1992).

After 5 ♘xd4 Black's main replies are **5...♘f6 (3.1)** and **5...♘c6 (3.2)**.

Rather slow is 5...a6 6 ♗d3 (if 6 exd5 Black can play 6...♕xd5! 7 ♘4f3 ♘f6 8 ♗c4 ♕c5 9 0-0 ♗d6 with easy development) 6...dxe4 7 ♘xe4 ♗e7 8 0-0 ♘f6 9 b3 ♘bd7 10 ♗b2 ♘xe4 11 ♗xe4 ♘f6 12 ♗d3 ♗c5 13 ♘f3 b6 14 ♕e2 ♗b7 15 ♖ad1 ♕e7 16 ♘e5± (Svidler-Speelman, Oviedo 1992).

3.1

(1 e4 e6 2 d4 d5 3 ♘d2 c5 4 ♘gf3 cxd4 5 ♘xd4)

5 ... ♘f6

6 ♗b5+ (3.11)
6 e5 (3.12)
6 exd5 (3.13)

6 Bd3?! e5 7 N4f3 dxe4 8 Nxe4
Nxe4 9 Bxe4 Wxd1+ 10 Kxd1 f6∓
(Zaichik-Glek, Philadelphia 1990).

We2 Wc7 14 Rac1 Rad8=
(Chiburdanidze-Nogueiras, Biel
1988).

3.11

(1 e4 e6 2 d4 d5 3 Nd2 c5 4 Ngf3
cxd4 5 Nxd4 Nf6)

6 Bb5+

6 ... Bd7
7 Bxd7+
(a) 7 We2 Wb6 (7...Bc5 8
Bxd7+ Nbxd7 9 N4f3 0-0-0=,
Schischke-Glek, Berlin 1990) 8 c3
Nxe4 9 Nxe4 dxe4 10 Be3 a6 11
Bxd7+ Nxd7 12 0-0 Wc7 13 Bg5
Bd6 14 h3 Nc5∓ (Sobeck-Nau-
mann, corr. 1992);
(b) 7 exd5 Bxb5 8 Nxb5 a6 9
Nc3 Nxd5 10 Nxd5 Wxd5 11 0-0
Be7= (Villarreal-Hmadi, Moscow
Olympiad 1994).
7 ... Nbxd7
8 exd5 Nxd5 9 0-0 Be7 10 c4
N5f6 11 b3 0-0 12 Bb2 a6 13

3.12

(1 e4 e6 2 d4 d5 3 Nd2 c5 4 Ngf3
cxd4 5 Nxd4 Nf6)

6 e5 Nfd7

7 N2f3
(a) 7 f4? Nxe5∓;
(b) 7 Bb5 Be7 (7...Wc7 8 Wh5?
g6 9 We2 Nc6 10 N2f3 Bg7 11
Bf4 0-0∓, Tkachiev-Kaidanov, New
York 1995; 8 N2f3) 8 Wg4 0-0 9
N2f3 f5 10 Wh5 Nc5 11 h4 Wc7 12
Bg5 Ne4∞ (Nikolenko-Glek, Moscow 1989).
7 ... Be7
7...Nc6:
(a) 8 Bb5 Wc7 (8...Wb6 9 0-0
Bc5 10 Be3 0-0 11 Bd3 Ncxe5 12
Nxe5 Nxe5 13 b4 Bxd4 14 Bxd4
Wc7 15 Bxh7+=, Shovikov-Zakh-
arov, Novgorod 1995) 9 0-0:

(a1) 9...a6 10 ♘xc6 bxc6 11 ♗a4 ♘c5 12 c3 ♘xa4 13 ♕xa4 ♗d7 14 ♖e1 c5 15 ♕g4± (Niko-lenko-Bus, Katowice 1993);

(a2) 9...♘cxe5 10 ♘xe5 ♕xe5 11 ♖e1 ♕f6 12 ♘f3⩱↑ (Nikolenko-S.Ivanov, Lubniewice 1994);

(a3) 9...♗e7!?∞;

(b) 8 ♘xc6 bxc6 9 ♗d3 ♗a6 10 0-0 ♗xd3 11 ♕xd3 ♗e7 12 c4 0-0 13 ♕c2 a5 14 ♖d1 a4 15 ♗f4 ♘b6 16 b3 c5= (Svidler-Dreev, Rostov 1993).

8   c3

8 ♗f4 ♕b6 9 c3 ♘c6 10 ♕c2 ♘c5 11 ♗e3 ♕c7 12 ♘xc6 bxc6 13 ♗xc5 ♗xc5 14 ♗d3 f5= (Schmitt-diel-Glek, Germany 1992).

8	**...**	**♘c5**
9	**♘b3**	**♘bd7**
10	**♗e2**	**0-0**
11	**0-0**	**f6**

11...♕c7!?

12	**exf6**	**♘xf6!**
13	**♗f4**	**♘g4**
14	**♕c1**	**♗d6**
15	**♗xd6**	**♕xd6 16 h3 ♖xf3=**

(Eingorn-Glek, Azov 1991) – *Game 5*.

3.13

(1 e4 e6 2 d4 d5 3 ♘d2 c5 4 ♘gf3 cxd4 5 ♘xd4 ♘f6)

6   exd5   ♕xd5

6...♘xd5 7 ♘2f3 – 1 e4 e6 2 d4 d5 3 ♘d2 c5 4 ♘gf3 ♘f6 5 exd5 ♘xd5 6 ♘b3 cxd4 7 ♘bxd4 (section 2.11).

7   ♘b5

7 ♘2f3 ♘c6=.

7   ...   ♘a6

7...♕d8 8 ♘c4 ♘d5 9 ♘e3 ♘c7 10 ♗d2 ♘xb5 11 ♗xb5+ ♗d7 12 ♗xd7+ ♕xd7 13 ♕g4 ♘c6 14 0-0-0 ♕d4 15 ♕e2 ♕a4 16 ♔b1 ♗e7 17 ♗c3 0-0 18 ♖d7± (Adams-Levitt, Dublin Zonal 1993).

8   ♗e2

8 ♘c4 ♕xd1+ 9 ♔xd1 ♗c5 10 ♘bd6+ ♔e7=.

8   ...   ♕xg2

8...♗d7 9 c4±.

9	**♗f3**	**♕g5**
10	**a4**	

10 ♕e2 ♗d7! 11 ♗xb7 ♗xb5 12 c4 ♖b8 13 cxb5 ♖xb7 14 bxa6 ♖d7∞ (S.Ivanov).

10   ...   ♕h4!

(a) 10...♕e5+ 11 ♔f1 ♘d5 12 ♘c4 ♕b8 13 ♗g5 h6?! (13...♗e7 14 ♗xe7 ♔xe7∞) 14 ♗h4 ♕f4 15 ♘cd6+ ♗xd6 16 ♗g3 ♕c4+ 17 ♗e2 ♕c6 18 ♘xd6+± (Yemelin-S.Ivanov, St Petersburg 1994);

(b) 10...♗c5 11 ♘e4 ♕e5 12 ♘bd6+ ♗xd6 13 ♕xd6 ♕a5+ 14 ♘c3 ♕b4 15 ♕g3!↑ (S.Ivanov).

11 ♕e2 ♗e7

△ ...0-0∞ (S.Ivanov).

3.2

(1 e4 e6 2 d4 d5 3 ♘d2 c5 4 ♘gf3 cxd4 5 ♘xd4)

5 ... ♘c6

6 ♘xc6 (3.21)
6 ♗b5 (3.22)

3.21

(1 e4 e6 2 d4 d5 3 ♘d2 c5 4 ♘gf3 cxd4 5 ♘xd4 ♘c6)

6 ♘xc6 bxc6
7 ♗d3 ♘f6

7...♗d6 8 ♕e2 ♕c7 9 b3 ♘f6?! (9...♗e5! 10 ♖b1 ♗c3∞) 10 ♗b2 ♗e5 11 ♗xe5 ♕xe5 12 0-0 a5 13 f4 ♕h5 14 ♖f3± (Hort-Wegener, Germany 1995) – *Game 6*.

8 0-0 ♗e7

8...♕b6 9 c4 ♗d6 10 ♕e2 ♕c7 11 cxd5 cxd5 12 ♗b5+ ♔e7 13 exd5 ♘xd5 14 ♘e4 ♗b7 15 ♘xd6 ♕xd6 16 ♕g4± (Zaltz-G.Gurevich, Israeli Ch 1992).

9	♖e1	0-0
10	c4	♗b7
11	e5	♘d7
12	♕g4	♗c8
13	♘f3	f5
14	exf6	♘xf6
15	♕g3	♗c5
16	♗e3	♗d6
17	♕h4	e5=

Fedorov-Wagner (Munich 1992).

3.22

(1 e4 e6 2 d4 d5 3 ♘d2 c5 4 ♘gf3 cxd4 5 ♘xd4 ♘c6)

6 ♗b5

6 ... ♗d7
7 ♘xc6

(a) 7 ♗xc6 bxc6 8 0-0 (8 c4 ♗d6=) 8...♗d6 9 ♕e2 ♕b8!? 10

♘4f3 ♘e7 11 e5 ♗c7= (Christian-sen-Yusupov, Munich 1992) – *Game 7*;

(b) 7 ♘4b3 ♘f6 8 exd5 ♘xd5 9 ♘e4 ♛c7 10 0-0 a6 11 ♗e2 ♗e7 12 c4 ♘f6 13 ♘g3 0-0-0 14 ♗e3 h5∞ (Papazov-Zalkind, Baile Herculane 1994).

7...bxc6 (3.221)
7...♗xc6 (3.222)

3.221

(1 e4 e6 2 d4 d5 3 ♘d2 c5 4 ♘gf3 cxd4 5 ♘xd4 ♘c6 6 ♗b5 ♗d7 7 ♘xc6)

7	...	bxc6
8	♗d3	

8	...	♛c7

(a) 8...♗d6 9 ♛e2 ♘e7 (9...e5 10 0-0 ♛e7 11 exd5 cxd5 12 c4±, Wolff-Finegold, St John 1988) 10 e5 ♗c7! 11 0–0 ♘g6 12 ♘f3 f6 Δ 13 ♗xg6+ hxg6 14 ♗f4?! g5 15 ♗g3 f5→;

(b) 8...♘e7 9 0-0 ♘g6 10 f4 ♗c5+ 11 ♔h1 0-0 12 ♛f3 dxe4 13 ♘xe4 ♗e7 14 ♗e3 ♛a5 15 ♛f2 ♖fb8 16 b3 f5 17 ♘d2± (Krays-Müller, Groningen 1994).

9	♛e2	♗d6

9...♘e7 10 ♘f3 ♘g6 11 0-0 ♗e7 12 c4 dxe4 13 ♗xe4 f5 14 ♗c2± (Shamkovich-Vaganian, Dubna 1973).

10	♘f3	dxe4
11	♛xe4	♘f6
12	♛h4	♘d5!

12...♖b8? 13 0-0 ♘d5 14 ♖e1 ♗e7 15 ♛g4 g6 16 c4± (Yudasin-Gulko, Biel Interzonal 1993).

13	0-0	♘b4
14	♖d1!±	

3.222

(1 e4 e6 2 d4 d5 3 ♘d2 c5 4 ♘gf3 cxd4 5 ♘xd4 ♘c6 6 ♗b5 ♗d7 7 ♘xc6)

7	...	♗xc6
8	♗xc6+	bxc6
9	c4	

9...dxe4 (3.2221)
9...♘f6 (3.2222)
9...♗c5 (3.2223)

9...d4?! 10 0-0 c5 11 f4±.

3.2221

(1 e4 e6 2 d4 d5 3 ♘d2 c5 4 ♘gf3
♘c6 5 ♗b5 cxd4 6 ♘xd4 ♗d7 7
♘xc6 ♗xc6 8 ♗xc6+ bxc6 9 c4)

| 9 | ... | dxe4 |
| 10 | ♕a4 | |

10 ♘xe4:

(a) 10...♕xd1+?! 11 ♔xd1 ♖d8+
12 ♔e2 ♖d4 13 ♘g5 ♖xc4 14 ♗e3
♗c5 15 ♖hc1 ♖xc1 16 ♖xc1 ♗xe3
17 fxe3 ♘e7 18 ♖d1∞ (Yemelin-
Y.Frolov, St Petersburg 1994);

(b) 10...♗b4+ 11 ♔e2 ♕a5 12
♗e3 ♗e7= (Van der Wiel-Ehlvest,
Naning 1990).

| 10 | ... | ♕b6 |
| 11 | ♘xe4 | ♗b4+ |

11...♕b4+ 12 ♕xb4 ♗xb4+ 13
♔e2 ♘f6 14 ♘xf6+ gxf6 15 ♗f4±
(Tal).

12	♔e2	♗e7
13	b3	♘f6
14	♘xf6+	♗xf6
15	♗e3	♕c7
16	♖ad1±	

Kholmov-Gavrilov (Moscow
1988).

3.2222

(1 e4 e6 2 d4 d5 3 ♘d2 c5 4 ♘gf3
♘c6 5 ♗b5 cxd4 6 ♘xd4 ♗d7 7
♘xc6 ♗xc6 8 ♗xc6+ bxc6 9 c4)

| 9 | ... | ♘f6 |

| 10 | ♕a4 | ♕d7 |
| 11 | e5 | ♘g4 |

11...♘g8 12 0-0 ♘e7 13 ♘f3±
(Oll-Rozentalis, Antwerp 1993).

| 12 | ♘f3 | ♖b8 |

12...♗c5 13 0-0 0-0 14 h3 ♘xf2
15 ♖xf2 f6 16 ♗f4 ♕c7 17 ♕c2±
(Kengis-Votava, Prague 1993).

13 a3   c5
14 ♕c2   ♗e7
15 h3   ♘h6
16 ♗xh6±

A.Kuzmin-Kholmov   (Moscow 1987).

3.2223

(1 e4 e6 2 d4 d5 3 ♘d2 c5 4 ♘gf3 ♘c6 5 ♗b5 cxd4 6 ♘xd4 ♗d7 7 ♘xc6 ♗xc6 8 ♗xc6+ bxc6 9 c4)

9   ...   ♗c5
10 ♕a4

10 cxd5 cxd5 11 exd5 ♕xd5 12 ♕a4+ ♕d7 13 ♕xd7+ ♔xd7 14 ♘b3 ♗b6 15 ♗f4 ♘e7= (Glek-Yusupov, Germany 1991).

10 ...   ♘e7
11 exd5   exd5
12 cxd5   ♕xd5
13 0-0   0-0
14 ♘e4   ♗d4
15 ♖d1   ♖fd8
16 ♗e3   ♘f5

17 ♘c3   ♕e5=

V.Ivanov-Pushkov (Russian Ch 1994).

Game 5
Eingorn–Glek
USSR 1991

1   e4   e6
2   d4   d5
3   ♘d2   c5
4   ♘gf3   cxd4
5   ♘xd4   ♘f6
6   e5   ♘fd7
7   ♘2f3   ♗e7
8   c3   ♘c5
9   ♘b3   ♘bd7
10 ♗e2   0-0
11 0-0   f6

The standard attack on the e5 pawn. With the pawn at f2, the weakness of the backward e6 pawn is illusory.

12 exf6   ♘xf6!
13 ♗f4   ♘g4

Now the rook comes into play.

14 ♕c1   ♗d6
15 ♗xd6   ♕xd6
16 h3   ♖xf3!
17 hxg4   ♖f7
18 ♕e3   ♘a4!

Now White cannot simultaneously defend his b2 pawn and prevent ...e6-e5.

19 c4!?   dxc4
20 ♘d2!   ♘xb2
21 ♖ab1   ♘a4
22 ♘xc4   ♕c5
23 ♕xc5   ♘xc5
24 ♖fd1

White's initiative fully compensates for the sacrificed pawn.

24	...	♖f8
25	♗f3	♖b8
26	♘e5	b6
27	♖dc1!	

27 ♘c6 ♖b7 is pointless.

27	...	♗a6
28	♘c6	♗d3?

This activity is inappropriate. Black was evidently aiming to avoid the draw by repetition after 28...♖b7 29 ♘b4 ♖bb8 30 ♘c6, but does he have anything better?

29	♖b4	♖be8
30	♘xa7	♖f7
31	♘c6	♘d7
32	♖d4	♗a6
33	♖cd1!	♘c5?

It was essential to return the bishop to its initial post by 33...♗c8.

34	♘e5	♖ff8
35	♖d6	♘a4?

Black lost on time

Game 6
Hort–Wegener
Germany 1995

1	e4	e6
2	d4	d5
3	♘d2	c5
4	♘gf3	cxd4
5	♘xd4	♘c6
6	♘xc6	

A problem for the theoreticians: which is better – to exchange immediately or after 6 ♗b5 ♗d7?

6	...	bxc6
7	♗d3	♗d6

A dubious idea, since all the same the knight will have to be developed at f6, when this bishop is more useful at e7. Therefore 7...♘f6 8 0-0 ♗e7 is usually played.

8	♕e2	♕c7
9	b3	♘f6?!

In view of the fact that the white bishops are aimed in the direction of the kingside, the development of the knight at e7 is too provocative, but why not make use of the opportunity to save a tempo: 9...♗e5! 10 ♖b1 ♗c3.

10	♗b2	♗e5
11	♗xe5	♕xe5
12	0-0	a5?!

A loss of time. 12...0-0 was better, and, if events had developed as in the game, Black would have gained an important tempo.

13	f4	♕h5
14	♖f3!	

14 ...   e5?!

For the exchange Black gives up too many pawns.

He should have reconciled himself to 14...0-0, and if 15 e5 ♘d7 16 ♕f2, then 16...f5, while after the cunning 15 ♕f1 (intending ♖h3) he has 15...e5 with the idea of 16 f5 ♕g5 17 ♖d1 ♘h5, when he can still hold on.

15 exd5!   ♗g4
16 dxc6   0-0
17 ♕xe5   ♗xf3
18 ♘xf3   ♖ac8

After 18...♖fe8 19 ♕xh5 ♘xh5 20 g3 ♖ac8 White would have retained his c6 pawn by 21 ♘e5 f6 22 ♗c4+ ♔f8 23 ♘d7+ ♔e7 24 ♗d5.

19 ♘d4   ♖fd8
20 c7!

This pawn is destined to decide the game. After the impulsive 20 c3 ♕xe5 21 fxe5 ♘d5 Black could have held on.

20 ...   ♖d5
21 ♕xh5   ♘xh5?

Black's last chance was to oppose the c7 pawn, which he should have attacked with his knight. Therefore correct was 21...♖xh5 22 ♘b5 ♖c5 (avoiding the threat of g2-g4 and ♗f5) 23 ♖e1 g6! followed by ...♘e8.

22 ♖e1   ♔f8
23 ♘b5   ♘xf4?

The same mistake; he should have returned the knight to f6, intending ...♘e8.

24 ♗f5!   ♘e6

The bishop is immune: 24...♖xf5 25 ♘d6.

25 ♗xe6   fxe6
26 c4   ♖d2
27 ♖xe6   g6

Now the pawn is immune: 27...♖xa2 28 ♘d6.

28 a4   ♖d3
29 ♖c6   ♔e7
30 ♖c5   ♖xb3

After 30...♔d7 White forces a won pawn ending: 31 ♖d5+ ♖xd5 32 cxd5 ♖xc7 33 ♘xc7 ♔xc7 34 ♔f2 ♔d6 35 ♔e3 ♔xd5 36 ♔d3 etc. But now he forces a won rook ending.

31 ♘a7   ♔d7
32 ♘xc8   ♔xc8
33 ♖xa5   ♖b4
34 ♖a8+   ♔xc7
35 ♖a7+   ♔b6
36 ♖xh7   ♖xc4
37 ♖h6   ♖c6
38 h4   ♔c7
39 ♔h2   ♔d7
40 a5   ♔e7
41 h5   ♖c5

| 42 | a6 | gxh5 |
| 43 | a7 | |

Black resigns

Game 7
Christiansen–Yusupov
Munich 1992

1	e4	e6
2	d4	d5
3	♘d2	c5
4	♘gf3	♘c6
5	♗b5	cxd4
6	♘xd4	♗d7
7	♗xc6	bxc6
8	0-0	♗d6
9	♕e2	♕b8!?

An original manoeuvre, setting up pressure on the b-file with gain of tempo. Less 'fresh' is 9...♘e7 10 e5 ♗c7 11 ♘2b3 etc.

10	♘4f3	♘e7
11	e5	♗c7
12	b3	

An unnecessary weakening, but Black has already solved his opening problems, and 12 ♘b3 can be met by 12...♕b5.

12	...	♘g6
13	♖e1	f6!
14	♗b2	0-0
15	c4	♗b6
16	♖ac1	♕e8

Black's initiative is associated with the f-file, but the direct 16...♘f4 17 ♕f1 ♕e8 is refuted by 18 c5 ♗c7 19 g3, while 16...fxe5 can be met by 17 c5 e4 18 cxb6 exf3 19 ♘xf3, when White's more active bishop, which has no opponent on the long diagonal, is sufficient compensation for the pawn. But perhaps 16...♖f7 followed by ...♕f8 would have been more cunning?

17	c5	♗c7
18	♘f1	♕f7
19	♕d2!	

Handing over the defence of the f2 pawn to the rook.

| 19 | ... | a5 |
| 20 | ♗d4! | |

Almost à la Nimzowitsch – over-protection of the f2 pawn, with the only difference that it is not strategically significant. But otherwise White's queen is overloaded, e.g. 20 a3 ♖ab8 21 b4 axb4 22 axb4 fxe5 23 ♘xe5 ♘xe5 24 ♗xe5 ♗xe5 25 ♖xe5 ♖xb4, and a pawn is lost.

20	...	♖ab8
21	♖c3	♖b4
22	♖ce3	♖xd4!

A spectacular exchange sacrifice, opening diagonals for the bishops. To avoid the worst, White is forced to reply in like fashion.

23	♕xd4	fxe5
24	♖xe5	♘xe5
25	♘xe5	♗xe5
26	♖xe5	♕f4

27 ♕b2?

With the given pawn structure the knight is stronger than the bishop, and this gives White a slight advantage, but Christiansen over-rates his chances. Yusupov suggests the following possibilities: 27 ♕e3! ♕xe3 28 ♖xe3 ♖b8 (the exchanging raid by the rook may end in White's favour after 28...♖f4 29 ♘d2 ♖d4 30 ♘f3 ♖d1+ 31 ♖e1 ♖xe1+ 32 ♘xe1) 29 ♘d2 ♖b5 30 ♖c3 ♔f7 (30...e5 31 ♘f3 e4 32 ♘e5! ♗e8 33 f3, or 30...a4 31 ♘f3 axb3 32 axb3 followed by ♘e5 and f2-f4 favours White) 31 f4 (not 31 ♘f3 ♔f6 32 ♘d4 ♖b4) 31...♖b4 32 g3 g5! 33 fxg5 e5 34 ♘f3 ♔e6, and the activity of the black pieces compensates for the sacrificed pawn.

27	...	♕b4
28	♕c1	♕d4

29 ♕e3   ♕a1!

The roles have been reversed, and now the active black queen avoids the exchange. This is natural, since White has too many problems: the pawns at a2, c5 and f2, plus the pin on his knight, which Black immediately emphasises.

30	♕e2	♗c8!
31	♖g5	

After 31 ♖e3 Black switches his attack to the c5 pawn – 31...♕c1!, but now he has a 'little' combination based on diverting the overloaded white queen.

31	...	♗a6!
32	♕xa6	♕f6
33	♕e2	♕xg5
34	♕xe6+	♔h8

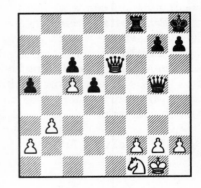

35 g3?

White is afraid of ghosts. After 35 ♕xc6 the passed c5 pawn would have given Black problems, for example: 35...♕f5 36 f3 ♖c8 37 ♕d6 d4 38 ♕xd4 ♕xc5 39 ♕xc5 ♖xc5 40 ♘e3, or 35...♕f4 36 f3

♕d4+ 37 ♔h1 ♕d1 38 ♔g1, when White can put up a tenacious defence. But now Black could have advantageously exchanged queens: 35...♕f6! 36 ♕xf6 ♖xf6 37 ♘d2 ♖e6, gaining real winning chances, since 36 ♕e3 would allow the d-pawn to advance with gain of tempo (Yusupov).

35	...	♕f5
36	♕e3	♖d8?!

Here too it was not yet too late for 36...♕f6!

37	♘d2	d4
38	♕e7	♖f8

After 38...♕d5 the knight also becomes active – 39 ♘e4!, with the threats of ♘d6 and ♘g5.

39	f4!	h6?!

39...♔g8! 40 ♘f3 ♕b1+ was more logical, not allowing White a respite. But now he succeeds in consolidating his forces and in neutralising Black's minimal material advantage.

40	♘f3	♕b1+
41	♔g2	♕c2+

After 41...♕xa2+ 42 ♔h3 ♖g8 43 ♘xd4 the important d-pawn would have been lost.

42	♔h3	♕f5+
43	♔g2	d3
44	♔f2	♖f7

45	♕e5	♕d7?!

Black misses what was probably his last chance: 45...d2! 46 ♕xf5 d1=♘+ 47 ♔e1 ♖xf5 48 ♔xd1 ♖xc5, when his rook is more active than in the game (Yusupov).

46	♕d6!	♕xd6
47	cxd6	♖d7
48	♘e5	d2
49	♔e2	d1=♕+
50	♔xd1	♖xd6+
51	♔e2	♔g8
52	a4	g5
53	♔e3	♔g7
54	♘c4?!	

A waste of an important tempo. 54 ♔e4 was correct.

54	...	♖d5
55	♘e5	gxf4+
56	♔xf4	♖d4+?

Black misses the opportunity for 56...♖c5 57 ♘c4 ♔f6, advantageously activating his king. Now the opposite happens.

57	♔f5!	♖b4
58	♘xc6	♖xb3
59	♘xa5	♖b4
60	♘c6	♖xa4
61	♘e5	♖a5
62	g4	♖a3
63	h4	♖h3
64	h5	♖g3
	draw agreed	

4

5 dxc5

1	e4	e6
2	d4	d5
3	♘d2	c5
4	exd5	♕xd5

By capturing the pawn with his queen, Black avoids the creation of an isolated pawn. And although the virtues of this are obvious, bringing the queen out early allows White to gain several tempi in development.

5 dxc5

A rare continuation, not without venom. Although the position is simplified, White still has resources to fight for the initiative.

The main move 5 ♘gf3 is covered in the remaining chapters of the book.

5	...	♗xc5
6	♘gf3	♘f6

For a long time 7 ♗c4 (4.1) was considered the main continuation, but in recent times 7 ♗d3 (4.2) has also begun to be employed.

4.1

(1 e4 e6 2 d4 d5 3 ♘d2 c5 4 exd5 ♕xd5 5 dxc5 ♗xc5 6 ♘gf3 ♘f6)

7	♗c4	♕h5

(a) 7...♕d8 8 ♕e2 0-0 9 ♘b3 ♗e7 10 ♗d2 a6 11 0-0-0 b5 12 ♗d3 ♗b7 13 ♘e5 ♗d5 14 f4± (Martinovic-Ornstein, Smederevska Palanka 1981);

(b) 7...♕c6 8 ♕e2 0-0 9 0-0 a6 10 ♘e5 ♕c7 11 ♘df3 (11 a4!?) 11...b5 12 ♗d3 ♗b7= (Kudryashov-Petrosian, Moscow 1967).

8	0-0	

8 b3 ♗b6 9 ♕e2 ♘c6 10 ♗e3 ♗xe3 11 ♕xe3 0-0 12 0-0 e5 13 ♖ae1 e4 14 ♘fd2 ♘e5 15 ♗e2 ♕g6∞ (Rubinchik-Glek, corr. 1988).

8	...	0-0
9	♕e2	♘bd7

9...♘c6 10 ♘e4 ♘xe4 11 ♕xe4 ♗d7 12 ♖d1 ♗e8 13 ♗f4 ♖c8 14 c3 ♘e7 15 ♘e5± (Serper-Huzman, Uzhgorod 1987).

10	♘e4	♘xe4
11	♕xe4	♗d6
12	♖e1	♘f6
13	♕h4	♕xh4
14	♘xh4	♗d7=

Gunawan-Klinger (Sarajevo 1988).

4.2

(1 e4 e6 2 d4 d5 3 ♘d2 c5 4 exd5 ♕xd5 5 dxc5 ♗xc5 6 ♘gf3 ♘f6)

7 ♗d3

White carries out a plan of attack on the kingside, castling on the opposite wing.

7 ... 0-0

7...b6 8 ♕e2 ♗b7 9 ♘b3 ♘bd7 10 ♗f4 a6 11 0-0-0 ♕h5 12 h3 ♗xf3 13 gxf3 ♘d5 14 ♗d2 0-0 15 c4 ♘e7 16 ♖hg1 ♘g6 17 ♔b1 ♖ad8 18 ♘xc5 ♘xc5∓ (Martinovic-Marjanovic, Yugoslav Ch 1986).

8 ♕e2 ♘bd7

8...♘c6 9 ♘e4 ♗e7 10 0-0±.

9 ♘e4 (4.21)
9 b3 (4.22)

4.21

(1 e4 e6 2 d4 d5 3 ♘d2 c5 4 exd5 ♕xd5 5 dxc5 ♗xc5 6 ♘gf3 ♘f6 7 ♗d3 0-0 8 ♕e2 ♘bd7)

9 ♘e4

9 ... b6!
10 ♘xc5 ♕xc5

10...♘xc5 11 ♗c4 ♕f5 12 ♗e3 ♗b7∞.

11 ♗e3 ♕c7
12 ♗d4 ♗b7
13 0-0-0 ♘c5!
14 ♗e5

14 ♗xf6 ♕f4+ 15 ♔b1 gxf6!?∞.

14 ... ♘xd3+
15 ♖xd3 ♕c4
16 ♘d4

16 ♘d2 ♕g4! (16...♕xa2 17 ♗xf6 gxf6 18 ♕g4+ ♔h8 19 ♕h4+) 17 f3 ♕g6 △ 18...♗a6, 18...♖ac8 (Anand).

16 ... ♗e4!
17 ♖e3 ♕xa2!
18 ♗xf6 ♗g6!
19 ♖a3 ♕d5
20 h4

20 ♗e5 f6!; 20 ♕e5 ♕xg2!∓.

20 ... gxf6
21 h5 ♕xd4
22 hxg6 hxg6

23	Qah3	f5
24	Qh4	f4
25	g3!	

25 Wf3? Qac8∓ (Kasparov-Anand, Reggio Emilia 1991/2).

25	...	Qac8
26	gxf4	Wf6
27	We5=	

(Anand).

4.22

(1 e4 e6 2 d4 d5 3 Ød2 c5 4 exd5 Wxd5 5 dxc5 Qxc5 6 Øgf3 Øf6 7 Qd3 0-0 8 We2 Øbd7)

9 b3

9 ... a5?!

(a) 9...Qb4 10 Qb2 Wc5 11 c4 Qa3 12 Qd4 Wc7 13 0-0 b6 14 Øe4± (Svidler-Lamoureux, Groningen 1993);

(b) 9...b6!? 10 Qb2 Qb7∞.

10	Qb2	b6
11	0-0-0	Qb7
12	g4!	

12 Qhe1 a4 13 Øe4 (13 Qe4! Øxe4 14 Øxe4 Wxe4 15 Wxe4 Qxe4 16 Qxe4 Qfd8 17 b4! Qe7 18 Qed4±) 13...Wh5 14 Øfg5 Wh6 15 ®b1 axb3 16 axb3 Qa3∓ (Rublevsky-Belyavsky, Novosibirsk 1995) – *Game 8*.

12	...	Wd6
13	g5	Ød5
14	We4→	

(Belyavsky).

Game 8
Rublevsky–Belyavsky
Novosibirsk 1995

1	e4	e6
2	d4	d5
3	Ød2	c5
4	exd5	Wxd5
5	dxc5	Qxc5
6	Øgf3	Øf6
7	Qd3	0-0
8	We2	Øbd7
9	b3	a5?!

9...b6 10 Qb2 Qb7 was better.

10	Qb2	b6
11	0-0-0	Qb7
12	Qhe1	

Belyavsky rightly considers that Black has more problems after 12 g4! Wd6 13 g5 Ød5 14 We4.

12	...	a4
13	Øe4	

White's last chance of maintaining the initiative was to go into the ending by 13 Qe4! Øxe4 14 Øxe4 Wxe4 15 Wxe4 Qxe4 16 Qxe4 Qfd8 17 b4! Qe7 18 Qed4 Øf6 19 Qxd8+ Qxd8 20 Qxd8+

♗xd8 21 ♘e5, when Black has
weak pawns at a4 and b6.

13	...	♕h5
14	♘fg5	♕h6
15	♔b1	axb3
16	axb3	

(*see diagram next column*)

16	...	♗a3!
17	♘xf6+?	

It is Black who now has the
initiative, and 17 ♗d4 was essential,
when he would have attacked with
17...♘d5!, with the idea of 18 ♘xh7
♖fc8, when 19...♗b4 is threatened.

17	...	♘xf6
18	♗xf6	♕xf6
19	♗xh7+	♔h8
20	♕h5?	♕b2 mate!

5

5 ♘gf3 cxd4 6 ♗c4 – Introduction

1	e4	e6
2	d4	d5
3	♘d2	c5
4	exd5	♛xd5
5	♘gf3	cxd4
6	♗c4	

White develops his bishop with gain of tempo, forcing the queen to move. However, the absence of pawn weaknesses leaves Black with hopes of successfully completing his development.

The main continuation is **6...♛d6** (Chapters 7-19), but also encountered from time to time is **6...♛d8** (Chapter 6), which appears equally logical, but which, in contrast to 6...♛d6, does not threaten to defend the d4 pawn (by ...e6-e5) and leaves White a wide choice of subsequent possibilities.

We should also mention the move **6...♛c5**, the only real justification for which is the element of surprise.

For example, in the event of 7 ♛e2 ♘c6 8 ♘e4?! he acquires the possibility of holding the pawn by 8...♛b6! 9 ♗f4 ♗d7 10 0-0-0 ♘f6 11 ♘e5 ♘xe4 12 ♛xe4 ♗d6! with a good game (Izeta-Kurajica, San Sebastian 1993).

But after the natural 7 0-0 ♘c6 8 ♛e2 ♛b6 9 ♘b3 Black has problems. Thus if 9...♘f6 10 ♖d1 ♗c5 there is the possibility of the flank attack 11 a4, which is also effective after 9...♘ge7 10 ♖d1 ♘f5 11 ♗d3 ♘d6 12 a4! Here are two examples:

(a) 12...a6 13 a5 ♛a7 14 ♖a4 ♘b5 15 ♗xb5 axb5 16 ♖axd4!± (Belyavsky-Nikolic, Wijk aan Zee 1984);

(b) 12...♘b4 13 a5 ♛c7 14 ♗f4 ♘xd3 (Kotronias-Popovic, Moscow 1989) 15 ♖xd3!±.

6...♕d8

1	e4	e6
2	d4	d5
3	♘d2	c5
4	exd5	♕xd5
5	♘gf3	cxd4
6	♗c4	♕d8

In the years immediately before and after the War this retreat was championed by the Swedish grandmaster Stahlberg. Since Black is not in a position to hold on to his pawn, White need not to hurry to regain it, but can choose the most comfortable way of developing, after first safeguarding his king.

7 0-0

Black's main reply is **7...♘c6 (6.1)**, but thanks to the efforts of grandmaster Dreev, an original plan of development beginning with **7...a6 (6.2)** has recently come onto the agenda.

7...♗c5?! 8 ♘b3 ♗b6 9 ♘bxd4 ♘e7 10 ♗e3 0-0 11 ♕e2 a6 12 ♖ad1 ♕c7 13 ♗d3 ♘bc6? (13...h6) 14 ♗xh7+!→ (Leu-Muck, corr. 1972).

6.1

(1 e4 e6 2 d4 d5 3 ♘d2 c5 4 exd5 ♕xd5 5 ♘gf3 cxd4 6 ♗c4 ♕d8 7 0-0)

7 ... ♘c6
8 ♘b3

8 ♘e4 a6 9 a4 ♘f6 10 ♘xf6+ gxf6 11 ♘h4?! f5 12 ♕h5 ♘e5 13 ♗g5 ♗e7 14 ♗xe7 ♕xe7∓ (Lane-Savchenko, London 1994).

8 ... ♘f6

8...♗e7 9 ♕e2 (9 ♘bxd4 ♘xd4 10 ♘xd4 a6 11 ♗e3±, Smyslov-Stahlberg, Helsinki Olympiad 1952) 9...♗f6?! (9... ♘f6!?) 10 ♖d1 a6 11 ♘bxd4 ♗xd4 12 ♗e3 ♘ge7 13 ♗xd4 ♘xd4 14 ♖xd4 ♕c7 15 ♖ad1 0-0 16 ♕e5± (Averbakh-Stahlberg, Stockholm Interzonal 1952).

9 ♕e2

White harmoniously develops his heavy pieces on the important central files.

9 ♘bxd4 ♘xd4 10 ♘xd4 is also possible, e.g. 10...a6 11 ♗f4 ♗e7 12 c3 0-0 13 ♕f3 ♕b6 14 ♗b3 ♗d7 15 ♖ad1 ♖fd8 16 ♖fe1 ♗c6 17 ♘xc6 bxc6 18 ♗e5± (Rublevsky-Thomsen, Moscow Olympiad 1994).

9 ...　　a6

9...♗d7 10 ♖d1 ♕c7 11 ♗g5 0-0-0 12 ♘bxd4 ♗c5 13 ♘b5 ♕b6 14 ♗f4 a6 15 ♗c7± (Sherzer-Lein, New York 1988).

10 ♖d1　　b5!?

10...♗e7 11 ♘bxd4 ♘xd4 12 ♖xd4 ♕b6 13 c3 ♗d7 14 ♘e5± (Mestel-T.Petrosian, Las Palmas Interzonal 1982).

11	♘bxd4	♘xd4
12	♖xd4	♕b6
13	♗d3	♗b7
14	a4	♗c5
15	♖h4	b4
16	a5	♕c7
17	♗d2±	

Sax-Andersson (Hilversum 1973) – *Game 9*.

6.2

(1 e4 e6 2 d4 d5 3 ♘d2 c5 4 exd5 ♕xd5 5 ♘gf3 cxd4 6 ♗c4 ♕d8 7 0-0)

7 ...　　a6

This prophylactic move is the start of an unusual plan of development, introduced in 1994 by Dreev. In his opinion the king's knight is badly placed at f6, since it has no good prospects there, and the best square for it is e7. From there it coordinates better with the other knight and can be played to a good post at g6, where it controls the important squares f4 and e5 with the support of the queen from c7.

The direct development 7...♘e7 8 ♘b3 ♕c7 9 ♕e2 (9 ♕xd4 ♘f5∓) 9...♘g6 runs into a strong initiative for White after 10 ♘bxd4! Forster-Vaganian (Biel 1994) continued 10...a6?! (10...♗e7 is safer) 11 ♗xe6! fxe6 12 ♘xe6 ♗xe6 (12... ♕e7 13 ♘c7+ ♔d7 14 ♕xe7+ ♗xe7 15 ♘xa8 ♗c5 16 b4!±) 13 ♕xe6+ ♕e7 (more cautious is 13... ♗e7 14 ♘g5 ♘c6! 15 ♕f7+ ♔d7 16 ♕f5+≅ – Forster) 14 ♕c8+ ♕d8 15 ♕xb7± with advantage to White.

It should be mentioned that White's first experience of this line proved less successful: 10 ♘fxd4?! a6 11 f4 ♗e7 12 f5 exf5 13 ♘xf5 ♗xf5 14 ♖xf5 0-0 15 ♘d4 ♘d7! 16 ♗e3 ♘f6 and Black firmly seized the initiative (Adams-Dreev, Dortmund 1994) – *Game 10*.

8 ♘b3

8 a4?! ♘c6 9 ♘b3 ♘f6 10 ♘bxd4 ♘xd4 11 ♘xd4 ♗d6 12 b3 (12 ♗d3!? 0-0 13 c3) 12...0-0 13 ♗b2 e5= (Tolnai-I.Almasi, Hungary 1995).

8 ... ♕c7

8...♘c6:

(a) 9 ♕e2 ♗d6 10 ♖d1 ♘ge7 11 ♘bxd4 ♘xd4 12 ♘xd4 ♕c7 13 ♗g5 ♗xh2+ 14 ♔h1 ♗f4 15 ♗b5+! axb5 16 ♘xb5 ♕e5 17 ♗xf4 ♕xf4 18 ♘d6+ ♔f8 19 ♕b5 ♘c6 20 ♘xb7∓→ (Acs-Tolnai, Budapest 1996);

(b) 9 ♘bxd4 ♘xd4 10 ♘xd4 ♗d6 11 ♗b3 (11 ♕g4!?; 11 ♗d3!?) 11... ♕c7 12 h3 ♘e7 13 c3 0-0 14 ♖e1 b6?! (14...e5!∞) 15 ♕h5 ♗b7? (15... ♘g6!) 16 ♖xe6!±± (Jansa-Thennhausen, Belgium 1995).

9 ♕e2

(a) 9 ♕xd4 ♘c6 10 ♕h4 ♗d6 11 ♗d2 ♘ge7 12 ♗d3 ♗d7 13 ♖ad1 0-0-0 14 ♘g5 ♘g6 15 ♕h5 ♘ge5 16 ♗e2 ♗e7∞ (Akopian-Dreev, Linares 1995);

(b) 9 ♗d3 ♘c6 10 ♘bxd4 ♘xd4 11 ♘xd4 ♗d6 12 h3:

(b1) 12...♘e7 13 ♖e1 0-0 14 ♕h5 ♘g6 15 ♘f3± (Adams-Dreev, London Rapid 1995);

(b2) 12...♘f6 13 c3 0-0 14 ♗g5 ♘d5 15 ♗c2 b5 16 ♘f5 ♗h2+ 17 ♔h1 ♗b7 18 ♘g3 ♗xg3 19 ♕d3 f5 20 ♕xg3 e5= (Hracek– Dreev, Brno 1994).

9 ... ♗d6

9...♘c6 10 ♖d1 ♗d6 11 ♘bxd4 ♘xd4 12 ♖xd4 ♘e7 13 a4 ♗d7 14 ♗d3 ♗c6 15 ♗e4± (Godena-Dreev, Reggio Emilia 1995/6).

10 ♘bxd4 ♘e7
11 ♖d1

11 ♖e1!? ♘bc6 (11...0–0? 12 ♘g5! [Δ ♘xe6] 12...h6 13 ♘xf7! ♔xf7 14 ♘xe6 ♗xe6 15 ♕xe6+ ♔e8 16 ♗xh6!±, Slobodjan-Kaminski, Halle 1995) 12 ♘xc6 ♘xc6 13 b3 ♗b4 14 ♗d2 ♗xd2 15 ♕xd2 0–0= (Faibisovich-A.Nikitin, St Petersburg 1995).

11 ... ♘bc6
12 ♗g5

12 ♘xc6!? – Dreev.

12 ... ♘xd4
13 ♘xd4 0-0
14 h3

14 ♗xe6?! fxe6 15 ♘xe6 ♗xh2+ 16 ♔h1 ♕e5! 17 ♕xe5 ♗xe5 18 ♘xf8 ♔xf8∓ (Zapata-Dreev, Wijk aan Zee 1995).

14 ... b5∞

Game 9
Sax–Andersson
Hilversum 1973

1	e4	e6
2	d4	d5
3	♘d2	c5

4	exd5	♕xd5
5	♘gf3	♘f6
6	♗c4	♕d8
7	0-0	cxd4
8	♘b3	♘c6
9	♕e2	a6
10	♖d1	b5
11	♘bxd4	♘xd4
12	♖xd4	♕b6
13	♗d3	♗b7
14	a4	♗c5
15	♖h4	b4
16	a5	♕c7
17	♗d2	

17 ♗f4 is well answered by 17...♗d6.

17	...	♘d5
18	♘e5	♕e7

This allows a tactical stroke. 18...♗e7 19 ♖g4 ♗f6 came into consideration.

19	♗b5+!	♔f8

After 19...axb5 20 ♕xb5+ ♔d8 21 ♖c4! White has a very strong attack, for example, 21...♖c8 22 ♖d1! f6 23 a6 ♗a8 24 ♗xb4! fxe5 25

♗a5+, or 21...♗d6 22 ♘c6+! ♗xc6 23 ♕xc6 ♖b8 24 a6! (Sax).

20	♖c4!	♗d6

Parrying the threat of 21 ♗xc5, but 20...f6 21 ♘d3 ♗xf2+ 22 ♕xf2 axb5 was also possible.

21	♗c6	♔g8
22	♖e1	♗xc6
23	♖xc6	h6
24	♘c4?!	

24 ♘f3 ♗c7 25 ♖a1 was more accurate, retaining slightly the better chances.

24	...	♗c7
25	♕e4	♕d7
26	♖c5	♖d8
27	g3	g6
28	♘e5	♗xe5
29	♕xe5	♔h7
30	♖e4	♖c8
31	♖h4	

A final attacking attempt.

31	...	h5
32	♗xb4	♘xb4
33	♖xb4	♖xc5
34	♕xc5	♖c8
	draw agreed	

Game 10
Adams–Dreev
Dortmund 1994

1	e4	e6
2	d4	d5
3	♘d2	c5
4	exd5	♕xd5
5	♘gf3	cxd4
6	♗c4	♕d8
7	0-0	♘e7

8 ♘b3   ♛c7
9 ♕e2

9 ♕xd4 is not good on account of 9...♘f5.

9 ...   ♘g6
10 ♘fxd4

This was the first occasion on which Dreev's variation was employed. It was later found that after 10 ♘bxd4! Black has problems.

10 ...   a6
11 f4   ♝e7
12 f5   exf5
13 ♘xf5   ♝xf5
14 ♖xf5   0-0
15 ♘d4?!

15 ♝d2 was stronger, with equal chances.

15 ...   ♘d7!
16 ♝e3

After the tempting 16 ♝xf7+ ♖xf7 17 ♖xf7 ♚xf7 18 ♕e6+ ♚f8 19 ♕xg6 hxg6 20 ♘e6+ ♚f7 21 ♘xc7 ♖c8 Black has the better endgame (Dreev).

16 ...   ♘f6
17 ♚h1   ♖ae8
18 ♕f1   ♘g4!

Black's initiative develops freely and naturally.

19 ♝g1   ♝f6
20 c3   ♘e3
21 ♝xe3   ♖xe3
22 ♝b3   ♖fe8
23 ♖f3

The attempt to seize the initiative with 23 ♖xf6 gxf6 24 ♘f5 is parried by 24...♖3e4! 25 ♘h6+ ♚g7 26 ♘f5+ ♚f8.

23 ...   ♖3e4!

It is important to retain control of the e-file, the main factor in Black's initiative. He is now threatening to play his knight via e5 to g4.

24 ♘f5?

It would have been useful to drive the rook away from e4 by 24 ♝d5 ♖4e5 25 ♝b3.

24 ...   ♘e5
25 ♖g3   ♘g4
26 ♖xg4   ♖xg4
27 ♘h6+   gxh6
28 ♕xf6   ♖ge4!

With this manoeuvre Black forces the exchange of a pair of rooks, in view of the possible pretty variation 29 ♖f1 ♖f4! 30 ♖xf4 ♕xf4 31 ♝xf7+ ♚f8!

29 ♖g1   ♖e1
30 ♕f2   ♖xg1+
31 ♚xg1   ♕e7
32 ♝d5   ♕e1+
33 ♕xe1   ♖xe1+
34 ♚f2   ♖e7
35 c4   ♚g7

36	b4	♔f6
37	♗f3	b6
38	a4	a5
39	bxa5	bxa5
40	c5	♖e5

41	c6	♔e7
42	h4	♔d6
43	h5	♖c5
44	♔e3	♖c4

White resigns

7　　6...♛d6 7 ♕e2

1	e4	e6
2	d4	d5
3	♘d2	c5
4	exd5	♛xd5
5	♘gf3	cxd4
6	♗c4	♛d6
7	♕e2	

This manoeuvre, preparing queenside castling, is one of the side lines of the main variation with 6...♛d6. The drawback to it is the fact that the temporary removal of the attack on the d4 pawn allows Black to support it by ...e6-e5 and to develop comfortably his queenside pieces.

A recent idea also comes into consideration: 7 ♗b3!? ♘f6 8 ♘c4 ♛d8 9 ♕xd4 ♛xd4 10 ♘xd4 ♗c5 11 ♘b5 ♘a6 12 ♗f4 0-0 13 ♘bd6 ♘c7 14 ♘xc8 ♖fxc8 15 ♘e5 ♘cd5

16 ♗g3 ♘e7 ½-½ (Topalov-Dreev, Wijk aan Zee 1996).

For the main move 7 0-0, see the following chapters.

7 ... ♘f6

7...♘c6 8 ♘e4 ♛c7 9 0-0 ♘f6 10 ♘xf6+ gxf6 11 ♖d1 ♗c5 12 a3 ♗d7 13 b4 ♗d6 14 ♗b2 ♘e5 15 ♗b3 ♗c6 16 ♘e1 ♖g8 17 g3 0-0-0∞ (Reinderman-Schwartzman, Wijk aan Zee 1994).

8 ♘b3 ♘c6

9 ♗g5 a6

(a) 9...♛b4+?! 10 ♗d2 ♛b6 11 0-0-0 ♗d7 12 ♗g5 0-0-0 13 ♘fxd4 ♘b4 (13...♘a5 14 ♘xa5 ♛xa5 15 ♗f4 ♘e8? 16 ♘xe6!±, Anka-Almasi, Budapest 1994; 15...♗e7±) 14 a3 ♘bd5 15 ♗xd5 exd5 16 f3 ♗d6 17 g3± (Rozentalis-Glek, Antwerp 1993);

(b) 9...♗e7!? 10 0-0-0 ♘d5!? 11 ♗xe7 ♛f4+ 12 ♔b1 ♘dxe7 13 ♘bxd4 0-0 14 g3 ♛c7 15 ♖he1 a6= (Losev-Danielian, Russia 1993).

10 0-0-0 b5

10...h6 11 ♘bxd4! (11 ♗xf6 ♛f4+! 12 ♔b1 ♛xf6 13 ♘fxd4 ♗d7=; 11 ♗h4 b5 12 ♗d3 ♗e7=) 11...hxg5 12 ♘xe6 fxe6 13 ♖xd6 ♗xd6 14 ♗xe6 ♔d8 15 ♛d2 ♘e4!∞ (Popovic-Bareev, Moscow Olympiad 1994) – *Game 11*.

11 ♗d3 ♗e7!

11...♗b7 12 ♘bxd4 ♘xd4 13 ♘xd4 0-0-0 (13...♛b6 14 f4!±) 14

♗xb5! axb5? (14...♕b6 15 ♕c4+
♗c5 16 b4±) 15 ♘xb5 ♕b4 16
♖xd8+ ♔xd8 17 ♖d1+ ♔c8 18 ♖d4
♕a5 19 ♕c4+ 1-0 (Smagin-Levitt,
Amantea 1993).

12   ♔b1

12 ♘bxd4 ♘xd4 13 ♘xd4 ♕d5
14 ♗xf6 ♗xf6 15 ♔b1 ♕c5! 16
♗e4 ♖a7 17 ♕d3 (V.Ivanov-
Zakharov, Russia 1994) 17...♖c7 18
♖he1 g6∓ (V.Ivanov).

12   ...   e5

12...♗d7 13 ♖he1 ♖d8 14 h4 h6
15 ♗c1 ♘d5 16 ♗e4 0-0 17 g3 e5
½-½ (Landenbergue-Hug, Horgen
1994).

13   h3   ♗e6
14   ♖he1   ♖c8!

15   ♗h4!

(a) 15 ♘xe5? ♕xe5 16 ♕xe5
♘xe5 17 ♖xe5 ♘d7∓;

(b) 15 g4 ♘d7∓ (Smagin-
Marjanovic, Yugoslavia 1994).

15   ...   ♘d7
16   ♗g3∞

(Smagin).

Game 11
Popovic–Bareev
Moscow Olympiad 1994

1	e4	e6
2	d4	d5
3	♘d2	c5
4	♘gf3	cxd4
5	exd5	♕xd5
6	♗c4	♕d6
7	♕e2	♘f6
8	♘b3	♘c6
9	♗g5	a6

Black prepares an offensive
against the king in anticipation of
10 0-0-0. The counter plan where he
also castles queenside 9...♕b4+ 10
♗d2 ♕b6 11 0-0-0 ♗d7 12 ♗g5
0-0-0 13 ♘fxd4 gives White the
better chances.

10   0-0-0   h6

11   ♘bxd4!

Black is obviously behind in
development, and White sacrifices
to expose the king, although the

resulting position with unbalanced material is by no means easy to evaluate. The exchange 11 ♗xf6 ♛f4+! 12 ♔b1 ♛xf6 13 ♘fxd4 ♗d7 would have made things easier for Black.

11	...	hxg5
12	♘xe6	fxe6
13	♖xd6	♗xd6
14	♗xe6	♔d8

To 14...♔f8 White has the good reply 15 g3 g4 16 ♘g5.

15 ♛d2

White moves out of a potential pin (15 ♛d1 ♔c7 with the idea of ...♖e8) and makes a real one, since 15...♔c7 can be met by 16 ♘xg5 ♖e8 17 ♖d1 with a continuing attack. But now too Black energetically completes his development.

15	...	♘e4!
16	♛d5	♗xe6
17	♛xe6	♖e8
18	♛f7!	

Otherwise after ...♔c7, and the inclusion of the second rook, White would be looking for a way to save the game.

18	...	♖e7

Black finds the only defence. After 18...g4? or 18...♖b8 White would have calmly continued the attack with 19 ♖d1.

19	♛f8+	♖e8
20	♛xg7	♖e7
21	♛g8+	♖e8
22	♛g7	♖e7
23	♛g8+	♖e8
24	♛g6	

White avoids the draw, since he is not convinced about the potential possibilities of the numerous black pieces.

24	...	♔c7
25	♖e1	♗f4+
26	♔b1	♖ad8
27	a3	♘c3+!
28	bxc3	♖xe1+
29	♘xe1	♖d1+
30	♔a2	♖xe1
31	h4!	
	draw agreed	

A draw from a position of strength. Naturally, the passed pawn cannot be taken on account of 31...gxh4?? 32 ♛f7+, but the consequences of 31...♖e2 32 g3 ♗e5 are also very difficult to evaluate.

8   7 0-0 ♘f6 8 ♘b3 ♘c6
9 ♕e2 and 9 ♖e1

1	e4	e6
2	d4	d5
3	♘d2	c5
4	exd5	♕xd5
5	♘gf3	cxd4
6	♗c4	♕d6
7	0-0	♘f6
8	♘b3	♘c6

In this chapter we will consider
9 ♕e2 (8.1) and **9 ♖e1 (8.2)**.

For the main continuation 9
♘bxd4, see the following chapters.

8.1

(1 e4 e6 2 d4 d5 3 ♘d2 c5 4 exd5
♕xd5 5 ♘gf3 cxd4 6 ♗c4 ♕d6 7
0-0 ♘f6 8 ♘b3 ♘c6)

9   ♕e2

The ideas involved with this
continuation have much in common
with the variations examined in the
previous chapter. By making the
thematic advance ...e6-e5, Black
successfully resolves his development problems.

We consider **9...a6 (8.11)** and
9...♗e7 (8.12).

9...♗d7?! 10 ♖d1 0-0-0 11
♘bxd4 ♘xd4 12 ♖xd4 ♕c7 13 ♗f4
♕b6 14 ♕e5 1-0 (Rozentalis-
Shulman, USSR 1986).

8.11

(1 e4 e6 2 d4 d5 3 ♘d2 c5 4 exd5
♕xd5 5 ♘gf3 cxd4 6 ♗c4 ♕d6 7
0-0 ♘f6 8 ♘b3 ♘c6 9 ♕e2)

9	...	a6
10	♖d1	

10 a4 ♗e7:

(a) 11 ♖e1 ♘d7 12 ♖d1 ♗f6 13
c3 ♘b6 14 ♘bd2 ♗e7 15 ♘e4 ♕c7
16 cxd4 0-0= (Bronstein-Lein,
USSR Ch 1967);

(b) 11 ♖d1 e5 12 h3 0-0 13 c3
♗e6! 14 cxd4 ♗xc4 15 ♕xc4 ♖ac8
16 d5 ♘d4 17 ♕d3 ♘c2∓∓ (Velim-
irovic-Popovic, Stara Pazova 1988);

(c) 11 ♗g5 e5 12 ♖fe1 ♗g4 13
h3 ♗xf3 14 ♕xf3 0-0 15 ♗h4 e4
16 ♕e2 ♖fe8 17 ♘d2 d3!∓

(Siklosi–Brink-Claussen, Copenhagen 1988);

(d) 11 g3 e5 12 ♘g5 0–0 13 f4 (Di Lao-Terenzi, 1991) 13...♗g4 14 ♘xf7 (14 ♕f2 e4!) 14...♗xe2 15 ♘xd6+ ♗xc4 16 ♘xc4 e4∓.

10	...	b5
11	♗d3	♕c7
12	a4	b4
13	♗c4	♗b7
14	♘bxd4	♘xd4
15	♖xd4±	

Geller-Dolmatov (Moscow 1992) – *Game 12*.

8.12

(1 e4 e6 2 d4 d5 3 ♘d2 c5 4 exd5 ♕xd5 5 ♘gf3 cxd4 6 ♗c4 ♕d6 7 0-0 ♘f6 8 ♘b3 ♘c6 9 ♕e2)

9	...	♗e7
10	♗g5	

10 ♖d1 e5 11 h3 (11 ♗b5 ♗g4 12 ♘bd2 ♘d7 13 h3 ♗xf3 14 ♘xf3 0-0 15 c3 ♗f6=, Lobron-Henley,

Indonesia 1983) 11...0-0 12 c3 ♗f5 13 cxd4 e4 14 ♘h2 a6 15 a4 ♗g6∞ (Istratescu-Zsu.Polgar, Budapest Zonal 1993).

10	...	0-0

10...e5!? 11 ♗b5 0-0 12 ♖fe1 e4 13 ♗xc6 bxc6 14 ♗xf6 ♗xf6 15 ♕xe4 ♗e6 16 ♘fxd4 ♗d5∞ (Zapata-Moran, New York 1993).

11	♖fe1	a6
12	♖ad1	b5
13	♗d3	♗b7
14	c3	♖ac8

14...♖fe8? 15 ♗b1± (Zapata-Dolmatov, Tilburg 1993).

15	♗b1	♖fd8
16	♘bxd4	♘xd4

17 ♘xd4 ♕c5 18 ♗e3 ♕c7 19 a3 ♘d5 20 ♗c1 ♗c5 ½-½ (A.Ivanov-Gulko, USA Ch 1994).

8.2

(1 e4 e6 2 d4 d5 3 ♘d2 c5 4 exd5 ♕xd5 5 ♘gf3 cxd4 6 ♗c4 ♕d6 7 0-0 ♘f6 8 ♘b3 ♘c6)

9   ♖e1

With this move White determines the position of his rook at an early stage, which in some variations where he plays his queen to f3 may simply transpose into the main variation (after 9 ♘bxd4 ♘xd4 10 ♘xd4). However, certain features of the position also allow Black to deploy his forces more successfully. One of his main resources is the preparation of counterplay on the b8-h2 diagonal.

We consider **9...♗e7 (8.21)** and **9...♗d7 (8.22)**.

9...a6:

(a) 10 a4 ♕c7 11 ♘bxd4 ♗d7 Δ ...♗d6 (Lane-Levitt, British Ch 1987);

(b) 10 g3 ♕c7 11 ♗f4 ♗d6 12 ♗xd6 ♕xd6 13 ♘bxd4 0-0 14 ♗f1 b5 15 ♗g2 ♗b7= (Ljubojevic-Speelman, Brussels 1988);

(c) 10 ♘bxd4 ♘xd4 11 ♘xd4 ♕c7 12 ♗d3 ♗d6 13 ♘f5 ♗xh2+ 14 ♔h1 ♔f8 15 g3 exf5 16 ♔xh2 ♗e6 17 ♕f3 h5 18 ♗f4 ♕b6 19

♗g5 h4 20 gxh4 ♕d4 21 ♗xf5 ♖xh4+∓ (Milov-Polak, Bern 1995).

8.21

(1 e4 e6 2 d4 d5 3 ♘d2 c5 4 exd5 ♕xd5 5 ♘gf3 cxd4 6 ♗c4 ♕d6 7 0-0 ♘f6 8 ♘b3 ♘c6 9 ♖e1)

9   ...   ♗e7
10   ♘bxd4   ♘xd4
11   ♘xd4

11 ♕xd4 ♕xd4 12 ♘xd4 ♗d7 13 ♗f4 ♖c8 14 ♗b3 ♖c5= (Capelan-Brunner, Solingen 1988).

11   ...   0-0

11...♗d7 12 c3 ♕c7 13 ♗b3 0-0 14 ♗g5 ♘d5= (Balashov-Spassky, Munich 1979).

12   c3

12 b3 e5 13 ♘f3 ♕xd1 (13...e4!? 14 ♕xd6 ♗xd6 15 ♘d4 a6=) 14 ♖xd1 e4 15 ♘e5 ♘g4∞ (Ljubojevic-Hübner, Tilburg 1986).

12   ...   ♗d7

12...e5!? 13 ♘f3 ♕xd1 14 ♖xd1 ♗g4∞.

13 ♕f3 ♕c7
14 ♗d3!
14 ♗b3 ♗d6! 15 h3 e5=.
14 ... ♗d6
14...♖fe8 15 ♗g5 (15 ♗f4!±)
15...♘d5 16 ♗xe7 ♖xe7! (16...
♘xe7 17 ♗xh7+! ♔xh7 18 ♕xf7→)
17 ♖ad1 ♗a4= (A.Sokolov-
Nogueiras, Brussels 1988);
15 h3 a6
16 ♗g5 ♗e5=
T.Horvath-I.Almasi (Hungary
1994) – *Game 13*.

8.22

(1 e4 e6 2 d4 d5 3 ♘d2 c5 4 exd5
♕xd5 5 ♘gf3 cxd4 6 ♗c4 ♕d6 7
0-0 ♘f6 8 ♘b3 ♘c6 9 ♖e1)

9 ... ♗d7

10 g3 ♗e7
10...♖c8 11 ♗f1 ♗e7 12 ♗f4
♕b4 13 a3 ♕b6 14 ♘e5 0-0 15 ♖c1
a5 16 ♘xc6 bxc6 17 ♕xd4 c5 18

♕c3 ♗d8= (Ljubojevic-Ehlvest,
Belfort 1988).
11 ♗f4 ♕b4
12 ♕d3 ♖c8
12...0-0 13 ♗c7 ♗d8 14 a3
♕e7= (Winsnes-Lein, Gausdal
1990).
13 a4 0-0
14 a5
14 ♗d2 ♕b6 15 ♘bxd4 ♘xd4
16 ♘xd4 ♖fd8= (Ljubojevic-
Nogueiras, Reggio Emilia 1985/6) –
Game 14.
14 ... ♗d8
14...e5 15 ♗xe5 ♗g4 16 ♘fd2±.
15 ♗d2 ♕d6
16 ♘bxd4 ♘xd4
17 ♘xd4 e5
18 ♘b5 ♕c5
19 b3 ♗g4
20 ♖e2 ♗xb5=
Ljubojevic-Nikolic (Tilburg
1987).

Game 12
Geller–Dolmatov
Moscow 1992

1 e4 e6
2 d4 d5
3 ♘d2 c5
4 exd5 ♕xd5
5 ♘gf3 cxd4
6 ♗c4 ♕d6
7 0-0 ♘f6
8 ♘b3 ♘c6
9 ♕e2 a6
10 ♖d1
10 a4 ♗e7 does not achieve
much for White.

10	...	b5
11	♗d3	♛c7
12	a4	

It is useful to weaken the c4 square.

12	...	b4
13	♗c4	♗b7
14	♘bxd4	♘xd4
15	♖xd4	♗c5

15...♗e7 was more prudent, since now Black does not manage to castle.

| 16 | ♖h4 | h5!? |

It was even more risky to castle into an attack after 16...0-0 17 ♗g5.

17	h3!	♘d5
18	♗g5	♗e7
19	♖d1	a5
20	♗b5+	

To 20 ♗xe7 Black has the good reply 20...♛xe7 (20...♘xe7?! 21 ♘e5 ♘f5 22 ♗b5+ ♔f8 23 ♖c4 is dangerous for him).

| 20 | ... | ♔f8 |
| 21 | ♖c4 | ♛d8 |

22   ♗xe7+?!

White should not have eased the defence by exchanging. 22 h4! was stronger, and if 22...♗xg5 23 hxg5!, while after the natural 22...♖c8 it is now good to play 23 ♗xe7+ ♔xe7 (or 23...♛xe7 24 ♖xc8+ ♗xc8 25 ♗c6, and the queen invades Black's rearguard) 24 ♘d4 ♔f8 25 ♘c6, retaining a dangerous initiative.

22	...	♛xe7
23	♘e5	♔g8
24	♘c6	

24 ♗c6 also came into consideration.

| 24 | ... | ♛f6 |
| 25 | ♖xd5? | |

This over-optimistic sacrifice is based on an oversight and it deprives White of the fruits of his efforts, whereas by increasing the pressure with 25 ♖c5 he would have retained the better chances. For example, 25...♛xb2?! can now be met by 26 ♖dxd5!

25	...	exd5
26	♘e7+	♔f8
27	♖c7	♖b8
28	♘c8	

It transpires that after 28 ♖xb7 ♖xb7 29 ♘g6+ ♔g8 30 ♛e8+ ♔h7 or 28 ♘g6+ ♛xg6 29 ♛e7+ ♔g8 30 ♖xb7 ♖xb7 31 ♛xb7 ♛xc2 Black defends successfully, retaining a big material advantage.

28	...	g6
29	♘e7	♔g7
30	c3	bxc3
31	bxc3	♛f4
32	♖d7	♖hd8
	White resigns	

	Game 13
	T.Horvath–I.Almasi
	Hungary 1994

1	e4	e6
2	d4	d5
3	♘d2	c5
4	♘gf3	cxd4
5	exd5	♕xd5
6	♗c4	♕d6
7	0-0	♘f6
8	♘b3	♘c6
9	♖e1	♗e7
10	♘bxd4	♘xd4
11	♘xd4	0-0
12	c3	♗d7

Black can also consider the more active development of his bishop by 12...e5 13 ♘f3 ♕xd1 14 ♖xd1 ♗g4.

13	♕f3	♕c7
14	♗d3!	♗d6

Or 14...♖fe8 15 ♗f4.

15	h3	a6

Now after 15...e5 16 ♘b5 ♗xb5 17 ♗xb5 White's two bishops ensure him the better chances.

16	♗g5	♗e5

A standard manoeuvre in this type of position. 16...♘d5 is weaker in view of 17 ♗e4!

17	♕e3	♗h2+
18	♔h1	♘d5
19	♕e4!	f5?!

A risky weakening of the position (19...g6 was more prudent), which White could have exploited by 20 ♕f3! ♗e5 21 ♖ad1, and now after 21...♗xd4 22 cxd4 he sets up pressure on the backward e6 pawn:

22...♖ae8 23 ♖e5 ♗c6 24 ♕e2 ♕f7 25 ♖e1, retaining the initiative.

20	♕e2	♖ae8
21	g3	

A tempting move, but 21 ♘f3 was somewhat better.

21	...	♗xg3
22	fxg3	♕xg3
23	♘f3	♕xh3+
24	♔g1	h6
25	♗d2	♗c6
26	♕g2	♕h5
	draw agreed	

	Game 14
	Ljubojevic–Nogueiras
	Reggio Emilia 1985/6

1	e4	e6
2	d4	d5
3	♘d2	c5
4	♘gf3	cxd4
5	exd5	♕xd5
6	♗c4	♕d6
7	0-0	♘f6

	8	♘b3	♘c6
	9	♖e1	♗d7
	10	g3	

An original plan for developing the dark-square bishop.

| | 10 | ... | ♗e7 |

10...♕c7 11 ♗f4 ♗d6 12 ♗xd6 ♕xd6 13 ♘bxd4 0-0 is also satisfactory.

	11	♗f4	♕b4
	12	♕d3	♖c8
	13	a4	0-0
	14	♗d2	♕b6
	15	♘bxd4	♘xd4
	16	♘xd4	♖fd8
	17	♗c3?!	

Allowing an unpleasant pin on the queen. 17 c3 was safer.

	17	...	♗c5!
	18	♗b3	♗e8
	19	♖ad1	♖d6
	20	♖d2!	♖cd8
	21	a5	♕c7
	22	♕c4	b5!
	23	axb6	♕xb6

| | 24 | ♘xe6! | |

A trick that enables White to escape from the seemingly mortal pin, since after 24...fxe6? 25 ♖xe6 ♗f7 26 ♖exd6! Black loses.

	24	...	♖xd2
	25	♘xc5	♖d1
	26	♘d3	♖xe1+
	27	♗xe1	♕b7
	28	♗a5	♖c8
	29	♕f4	♗c6

Black tries to extract something from the long diagonal, but 29...♕e4!? would perhaps have been simpler.

	30	♗c3	♘d5
	31	♗xd5	♗xd5
	32	♕g5?	

Missing a tactical opportunity to win a pawn: 32 ♘c5! ♕c6 (32...♖xc5? 33 ♕d4) 33 ♕g4 f6 34 ♗xf6.

| | 32 | ... | f5?! |

Black in turn goes wrong, after which the battle for control of the long diagonals turns in White's favour. After 32...f6! 33 ♗xf6 h6 he would have stood badly.

	33	♕e3	♗f7
	34	♕e5	♗c4

An admission of the obvious – Black aims for the exchange of the knight, after which the remaining white bishop is in no way inferior to the rook.

	35	♕xf5	♖f8
	36	♕c5	♗xd3
	37	cxd3	h6
	38	h4	♖f7
	39	♗e5	♕f3
	40	♕c2	♕f5

41	♕e2	♖e7		47	♗f4	♕g6
42	d4	♔h7		48	♕c5	♕e4+
43	♔g2	h5		49	♔g1	♕e1+
44	♕f3	♔g6		50	♔g2	♕e4+
45	♕c6+	♔h7		51	♔g1	
46	b4	♖f7			draw agreed	

9 9 ♘bxd4 ♘xd4 10 ♛xd4

1	e4	e6
2	d4	d5
3	♘d2	c5
4	exd5	♛xd5
5	♘gf3	cxd4
6	♗c4	♛d6
7	0-0	♘f6
8	♘b3	♘c6
9	♘bxd4	♘xd4
10	♛xd4	

The main line 10 ♘xd4 is covered in the remaining chapters of the book.

When playing the variation with 4...♛xd5 Black must also be prepared for the complicated ending, arising after the exchange of queens. It has to be said that his problems are not so simple as might appear at first sight. Here too White's lead in development is significant.

Black's main continuations are 10...♛xd4 (9.1) and 10...♗d7 (9.2).

9.1

(1 e4 e6 2 d4 d5 3 ♘d2 c5 4 exd5 ♛xd5 5 ♘gf3 cxd4 6 ♗c4 ♛d6 7 0-0 ♘f6 8 ♘b3 ♘c6 9 ♘bxd4 ♘xd4 10 ♛xd4)

10 ... ♛xd4

After the direct exchange of queens White has better chances of developing an attack on the queenside, and therefore in recent times the preparatory 10...♗d7 has been considered more flexible.

11 ♘xd4

11 ... a6

This move, planning to develop the light-square bishop by the extended fianchetto, is considered

Black's main resource, although it weakens his queenside, making it easier for White to attack it. 11...♗d7 is also very popular, transposing to 9.22 after 12 ♗f4 or 9.23 after 12 ♗e2.

11...♗e7, with which Black aims to complete his development as quickly as possible, also comes into consideration.

With 'lethargic' play White can hardly count on an advantage, for example: 12 b3 0-0 13 ♗b2 ♗d7 14 ♖fd1 ♖fd8 15 ♗e2 ♗e8= (Glek-Rubinchik, corr. 1986-8), or 12 c3 0-0 13 a4 ♗d7 14 ♗b5 ♖fd8 15 ᐁb3 a6= (Reiter-Hoang, Budapest 1994).

12 ♗f4!? (with the threat of ᐁb5) would seem to be more active, when after 12...♗d7 13 ♖ad1 White retains the better chances.

12 ♗f4

(a) 12 ♖e1 ♗d7 13 ♗g5 ♖c8 14 ♗b3 h6 15 ♗h4 ᐁh5= (Saltaev-Dokhoyan, Sevastopol 1986);

(b) 12 ♗e2 ♗d7 13 ♗f3 0-0-0 14 ♗f4 ♗a4 15 ᐁb3 ♗xb3 16 axb3 ♗d6= (Sherzer-Bonin, New York 1987);

(c) 12 a4 ♗d6 (12...♗e7!?) 13 ♖e1 0-0 14 ♗g5 ᐁd5 15 ♖ad1 ♗e7 16 ♗xe7 ᐁxe7 17 a5 ♖d8 18 ᐁf5 ᐁc6 19 ᐁe7+! ♔f8 20 ᐁxc6 ♖xd1 21 ♖xd1± (Fiello-C.Santos, Moscow Olympiad 1994).

12 ...   b5

(a) 12...♗c5 13 ᐁb3:

(a1) 13...♗e7 14 ♗e2 ᐁd5 15 ♗g3 ♗d7 16 ♗f3 (16 ♖fd1 ᐁb4 17 c3 ᐁc6 18 ♗f3 f6 19 ♗c7±,

Gelfand-Orlov, USSR 1986) 16... ♗c8 17 c3 0-0 18 ♖fd1± (Gipslis-Uhlmann, Moscow 1967) – *Game 15*;

(a2) 13...♗b6 14 ♗e2 (14 ♗d6!? ♗d7 15 ♖ad1 ♗c6 16 ♗a3±) 14...♗d7 15 ᐁd2 ᐁd5 16 ♗g3 ᐁe3 17 ♖fc1 ♗c6= (Rasik-I.Sokolov, Debrecen 1992);

(b) 12...♗d7 13 ♗e2 0-0-0 (13...ᐁd5 14 ♗g3 ♗c5 15 ♖fd1±, Van der Wiel-Chernin, Wijk aan Zee 1986) 14 ♗f3 ♗c5 15 ᐁb3 ♗b6 16 ♖fe1 ♗a4= (Relange-Danielian, Cannes 1993);

(c) 12...♗e7 13 a4 (13 ♗e2!? Δ ♗f3±) 13...0-0 14 ♖fe1 ♖d8 15 c3 ᐁd5 16 ♗g3 ♗f6 17 ♗e5± (Hutcheson-Melas, Moscow Olympiad 1994).

13 ♗e2

13 ♗b3 ♗c5 14 ♖ad1 ♗b7 15 ♗e3 ♖c8 (15...0-0-0 16 ᐁf5?! ♗xe3 17 ᐁxe3 ᐁe4! 18 ♖xd8+ ♖xd8 19 ♖d1 ♖xd1+ 20 ᐁxd1 ᐁd2∓, Prandstetter-Ornstein, Skara 1980)

16 ♖fe1 ♗d5= (Tiviakov-Wieden-keller, Stockholm 1990).

13 ...   ♗b7
14 ♘b3

(a) 14 a4 b4 15 ♘b3 ♗e7 16 ♘a5 ♗e4∓ (Kaminski-Gebhardt, Dortmund 1992);

(b) 14 ♗f3 ♗xf3 15 ♘xf3 ♘d5 16 ♗d2 ♗e7 17 ♘e5 ♖c8= (Witt-mann-Villamayor, Moscow Olympiad 1994);

(c) 14 c3 ♘d7! 15 ♗g3 ♘c5= (Rizzitano).

14 ...   ♗d5

14...♗e7 15 c4 bxc4 16 ♘a5 ♗d5 17 ♘xc4 ♗c5 18 ♖ac1 0-0 19 a3 a5 20 ♘xa5± (Hübner-Klinger, Biel 1986).

15 a4   b4
16 a5   ♗e7
17 ♘d2?!

17 ♗e3!? △ ♘c5∞.

17 ...   0-0
18 ♘c4   ♖ac8
19 ♘b6

19 b3 ♘e4!

19 ...   ♖xc2∓

Wessman-Wiedenkeller (Swedish Ch 1989).

9.2

(1 e4 e6 2 d4 d5 3 ♘d2 c5 4 exd5 ♕xd5 5 ♘gf3 cxd4 6 ♗c4 ♕d6 7 0-0 ♘f6 8 ♘b3 ♘c6 9 ♘bxd4 ♘xd4 10 ♕xd4)

10 ...   ♗d7

Black delays the exchange of queens, inviting White to declare his intentions. His main contin-uations are **11 ♗e3 (9.21)**, **11 ♗f4 (9.22)** and **11 ♗e2 (9.23)**.

After 11 ♗g5 ♕xd4 12 ♘xd4 ♘e4! 13 ♗e3 ♖c8 14 ♗e2 ♗c5 15 c3 ♘d6 16 ♖ad1 ♔e7 Black easily maintains the balance (Sosna-Glek, Linz 1989).

9.21

(1 e4 e6 2 d4 d5 3 ♘d2 c5 4 exd5 ♕xd5 5 ♘gf3 cxd4 6 ♗c4 ♕d6 7 0-0 ♘f6 8 ♘b3 ♘c6 9 ♘bxd4 ♘xd4 10 ♕xd4 ♗d7)

11 ♗e3

After this move Black is again not forced to exchange queens, but can use the important tempo for the development of his rook. It would seem that White can hardly count on gaining an advantage in this way.

11 ...   ♖c8

11...a6 12 a4 ♕xd4 13 ♗xd4 ♖c8 14 ♗b3 ♗c5 15 ♖fd1 ♔e7 16

♘e5 Ihd8 17 ♘xd7 ♗xd4 18 ♘xf6 ♗xf6= (Rodriguez-Djurhuus, Santiago 1990).

12	♘e5	♕xd4
13	♗xd4	♗c5
14	Iad1	

14 Ifd1 ♔e7 15 ♘xd7 ♗xd4 16 Ixd4 ♘xd7 17 Iad1 ♘e5!? 18 ♗b3 Ihd8= (Seger-Rosenthal, Germany 1993).

14	...	♔e7
15	♘xd7	♗xd4
16	Ixd4	Ihd8!

16...♘xd7 17 Ifd1 Ihd8 18 f4± (Brodsky-Glek, Katowice 1992).

17	Ifd1	Ixd7
18	Ixd7+	♘xd7

19 ♗b5 ♘e5 20 c3 a6 21 ♗e2 ♘c4= (Brodsky).

9.22

(1 e4 e6 2 d4 d5 3 ♘d2 c5 4 exd5 ♕xd5 5 ♘gf3 cxd4 6 ♗c4 ♕d6 7 0-0 ♘f6 8 ♘b3 ♘c6 9 ♘bxd4 ♘xd4 10 ♕xd4 ♗d7)

11 ♗f4

Forcing Black to make up his mind, but as in the previous variation he regains an important tempo by attacking the bishop at c4.

11	...	♕xd4
12	♘xd4	

12 ... Ic8

(a) 12...♗e7 13 Iad1 (13 Ife1 Ie8 14 ♗b3 Ic5=, T.Horvath-Adorjan, Reykjavik 1982) 13...0-0 14 ♗e2 Iac8 15 c4 Ifd8 16 b3± (Spasov-Tal, Manila 1990) – *Game 16*;

(b) 12...0-0-0 13 Iad1 ♗c5 14 Id3 ♗a4!? 15 Ifd1 ♗xd4 16 Ixd4 Ixd4 17 Ixd4 Id8 (17...♗xc2 18 ♗xe6+±) 18 Ixd8+ ♔xd8 19 ♗d3 h6 20 ♗e5± (Prandstetter-Keitlinghaus, Prague 1990).

13 ♗e2

13 ♗b3 ♘e4 (13...♗c5 14 Iad1 0-0 15 Ife1 Ifd8 16 ♗g5 ♗e8=, Rozentalis-Kruppa, Uzhgorod 1987) 14 Ifd1 ♘c5 15 Id2 ♗e7 16 c3 f6 17 ♗e3 e5= (Eismont-Glek, Katowice 1993).

13...♗c5 (9.221)
13...♘d5 (9.222)

9.221

(1 e4 e6 2 d4 d5 3 ♘d2 c5 4 exd5
♕xd5 5 ♘gf3 cxd4 6 ♗c4 ♕d6 7
0-0 ♘f6 8 ♘b3 ♘c6 9 ♘bxd4
♘xd4 10 ♕xd4 ♗d7 11 ♗f4 ♕xd4
12 ♘xd4 ♖c8 13 ♗e2)

13	...	♗c5
14	♘b3	

14	**...**	**♗b6**

14...♗e7:

(a) 15 c3 0-0 16 ♖fd1 ♖fd8 17
♗e3 a6 18 ♘a5± (Shchekachev-
Gutop, Moscow 1987);

(b) 15 c4 0-0 16 ♗e3 (16 ♖ac1
b6 17 c5 bxc5 18 ♗e3 ♖b8 19
♘xc5 ♖xb2 20 ♘xd7 ♘xd7 21
♖c7∞, Marjanovic-Stanojevic, Kis
1994) 16...b6 17 a4± (Istratescu-
Navrotescu, Romanian Ch 1992).

15   c3

15 c4 ♘e4 16 ♖ac1 ♔e7 17 ♗f3
♗c6= (Müller-Bus, Oakham 1992).

15	...	♔e7
16	a4	a6
17	a5	♗a7
18	♖fd1	♖hd8
19	♘d4	♗e8
20	♗e3	♗c5
21	♗f3	♘d5=

Istratescu-Huzman (Biel 1993).

9.222

(1 e4 e6 2 d4 d5 3 ♘d2 c5 4 exd5
♕xd5 5 ♘gf3 cxd4 6 ♗c4 ♕d6 7
0-0 ♘f6 8 ♘b3 ♘c6 9 ♘bxd4
♘xd4 10 ♕xd4 ♗d7 11 ♗f4 ♕xd4
12 ♘xd4 ♖c8 13 ♗e2)

13	...	♘d5
14	♗g3	

14	**...**	**h5!?**

14...♗c5 15 ♘b3 ♗b6 (15...♗e7
16 c4 ♘f6 17 ♖fd1 0-0 18 ♘d4
♖fd8 19 ♖ac1 ♘e4 20 ♗f4 ♗f6 21
♗e3±, Yang-Hutcheson, Manila

Olympiad 1992) 16 c4 ♘e7 17 ♖fd1 ♘f5 18 ♗e5 f6 19 ♗c3 h5= (Womacka-Luther, Dresden 1987).

15 c4

15 h4 ♗c5 16 ♘b3 ♗b6 17 c3 ♗c7= (Kaminski-Glek, Cham 1993).

15 ... h4
16 cxd5 hxg3
17 hxg3 e5!
18 ♘f3 ♗d6=

Womacka-Glek (Cattolica 1993).

9.23

(1 e4 e6 2 d4 d5 3 ♘d2 c5 4 exd5 ♕xd5 5 ♘gf3 cxd4 6 ♗c4 ♕d6 7 0-0 ♘f6 8 ♘b3 ♘c6 9 ♘bxd4 ♘xd4 10 ♕xd4 ♗d7)

11 ♗e2

The most popular move. White withdraws his bishop in advance, inviting Black to take a decision. It would seem that he can avoid the immediate exchange of queens: 11...♕c7 12 c4 ♗c5 13 ♕h4 h6 14

♗f4 ♗d6 15 ♗xd6 ♕xd6 16 ♖fd1 ♕c7 17 ♕g3 ♕xg3 18 hxg3 ♔e7= (Van der Wiel-Glek, Tilburg 1994). The alternative is the immediate exchange, by which Black gains the opportunity to develop his second bishop more actively.

11 ... ♕xd4
12 ♘xd4 ♗c5
13 ♘b3 ♗b6

13...♗d6 14 ♖d1 ♔e7 15 ♗f3 ♖ac8 16 c3 b6 17 ♗g5 ♖hd8= (Landenbergue-Guliev, Moscow Olympiad 1994).

14 a4

14 ♗f4 0-0-0 15 c4 ♗c6 16 c5 ♗c7 17 ♗xc7 ♔xc7 18 ♖fd1 ♗a4∓ (Müller-Luce, Cappelle la Grande 1993).

14 ... a6
15 ♗f3 0-0-0
16 ♗d2

16 ♖e1 ♘d5 17 ♗g5± (Van der Wiel-Andersson, Reggio Emilia 1986/7).

16 ... ♗c6!

16...e5 17 ♗c3 ♖he8 18 ♖fe1±.

17 ♗xc6 bxc6
18 ♗c3±

Tiviakov-Chernin (Podolsk 1993) – *Game 17.*

Game 15
Gipslis–Uhlmann
Moscow 1967

1	e4	e6
2	d4	d5
3	♘d2	c5
4	♘gf3	cxd4

5	exd5	♕xd5
6	♗c4	♕d6
7	0-0	♘f6
8	♘b3	♘c6
9	♘bxd4	♘xd4
10	♕xd4	♕xd4
11	♘xd4	a6
12	♗f4	♗c5

More in the spirit of the 11...a6 variation is the extended fianchetto after 12...b5. However, Black wants to avoid weakening his queenside, but agrees to develop his bishop at e7 only after driving back the knight.

13	♘b3	♗e7
14	♗e2	

Preventing 14...b5? on account of 15 ♗f3 ♖a7 16 ♗b8.

14	...	♘d5

14...♗d7 15 ♗f3 ♖c8 16 c3 ♗c6 would seem to be more accurate, since now almost by force White weakens Black's queenside pawns and gains the better chances.

15	♗g3	♗d7
16	♗f3	♖c8
17	c3	0-0
18	♖fd1	

18 ♗xd5 exd5 19 ♖ac1 ♗e6 20 ♘d4 is also good.

18	...	♗c6
19	♘a5	♗f6

19...f5 would have been met with 20 ♗e5 followed by 21 ♘xc6.

20	♘xc6	bxc6
21	♖d3	g6
22	♔f1	h5?!

A loss of time. The prophylactic 22...♖fe8 was better.

23	♖ad1	♖fe8
24	♗d6	a5

If 24...♗e7 25 ♗xe7 ♖xe7 there would have followed 26 c4, with a decisive rook invasion on the d-file.

25	c4	♘b4
26	♖a3	♖a8
27	b3!	

The start of an operation to encircle the knight.

27	...	♗e7
28	♗xe7	♖xe7
29	♖a4!	♖aa7
30	h4	♔g7
31	♖d2	

For the moment 31 a3 is premature in view of the possible boomerang against the rook at a4: 31...♘a2! 32 ♖d3 c5 with the threat of ...e6-e5.

31	...	♖ed7

32 ♖xd7 ♖xd7 33 a3 ♘d3 34 ♖xa5 c5 35 ♖b5 ♖d4 36 a4 e5 37 a5 e4 38 ♗e2 ♘c1 39 ♔e1 ♖d7 40 ♖xc5 ♘xb3 41 ♖b5 ♘c1 42 a6 **Black resigns**

```
        Game 16
      Spasov–Tal
  Manila Interzonal 1990
```

1	e4	e6
2	d4	d5
3	♘d2	c5
4	♘gf3	cxd4
5	exd5	♕xd5
6	♗c4	♕d6
7	0-0	♘f6
8	♘b3	♘c6
9	♘fxd4	♘xd4
10	♕xd4	♕xd4
11	♘xd4	♗d7
12	♗f4	♗e7

The more active 12...♖c8 is more usual, but Black also has a quite sound position after the modest development of his second bishop.

13	♖ad1	0-0
14	♗e2	♖ac8
15	c4	♖fd8
16	b3	♖c5
17	♗e3	♖cc8
18	♗f4	♖c5
19	♖fe1!	

A tactical way of controlling the important e5 square, since 19...e5? is met by 20 ♗f3! ♗d6 21 ♗g3! (but not 21 ♘c2? ♗f5!). Black is therefore forced to wait, and White can gradually improve the placing of his pieces, choosing a convenient moment to go onto the offensive.

19	...	♗e8
20	♗f3	b6
21	h3	♖d7
22	a4	♖c8
23	♘b5	a5
24	♖xd7	♗xd7
25	♘d6	♗xd6
26	♗xd6	♗c6
27	♗xc6	♖xc6
28	♗e7	♘e8?

It is out of such 'trifles' that problems are aggravated. It was no longer feasible to wait, and Black should have actively opposed the bishop with 28...♖c7! 29 ♗d8 (29 ♗a3 is adequately met by 29...♘d7) 29...♖c8 30 ♖d1 ♔f8.

29	♖d1!	♖c7
30	♗a3	

The difference compared with the previous note is obvious: White has complete control of the d-file, along which he can approach the b6 pawn.

30	...	f6
31	♖d8	♔f7
32	♖b8	♖c6
33	♗c1	♘d6
34	♗e3	♘xc4

Sacrifices of this type are made out of desperation. After the passive 34...♘c8 35 ♖b7+ ♔g6 36 ♔f1

White increases his advantage by bringing his king into the game. But now it is merely a matter of technique.

35 bxc4 Rxc4 36 Rb7+ Kg8 37 Rxb6 e5 38 Rb8+ Kf7 39 Rb7+ Kg8 40 Ra7 Rxa4 41 g3 Ra1+ 42 Kg2 a4 43 Bc5 Rc1 44 Bb4 Ra1 45 h4 h5 46 Kf3 Ra2 47 Ke3 Ra1 48 Ke4 Rd1 49 Bc5 Rc1 50 Kd5 Rd1+ 51 Ke6 Rc1 52 Be7 Rc4 53 Ra8+ Kh7 54 Kf7 Black resigns

---

Game 17
Tiviakov–Chernin
Podolsk 1993

1	e4	e6
2	d4	d5
3	Nd2	c5
4	exd5	Qxd5
5	Ngf3	cxd4
6	Bc4	Qd6
7	0-0	Nf6
8	Nb3	Nc6
9	Nbxd4	Nxd4
10	Qxd4	Qxd4
11	Nxd4	Bd7
12	Be2	Bc5
13	Nb3	Bb6
14	a4	a6
15	Bf3	0-0-0
16	Bd2	

White transfers his bishop to the long diagonal, but 16 Re1 Nd5 17 Bg5 is also good.

16	...	Bc6!
17	Bxc6	bxc6
18	Bc3	Rhg8

Black defends his g7 pawn. After the more active 18...Rd5 he has to reckon with play against other weak points in his position: 19 Nd2! Bd4 (or 19...Rhd8 20 Nc4 Bc7 21 Rfe1, intensifying the pressure) 20 Bxd4 Rxd4 21 Nf3 Rd5 22 Rfe1 followed by Ne5.

19	Rfe1	Rd5
20	Nd2	Ng4

Black is not agreeable to the complete passivity that would await him after 20...Bd4 21 Bxd4 Rxd4 22 Nf3.

21	Re2	Rgd8
22	Rf1	Bd4
23	Nc4	

A tactical trick – 23...Bxc3? 24 Nb6+.

23	...	Rc5
24	Bxd4	Rxd4
25	b3	

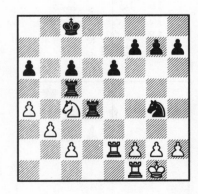

25	...	Rcxc4!?

The modern style of defence! It is easier to resist with a minimal material deficit than in the completely passive position after 25...♔c7 26 h3 ♘f6 27 ♘e5.

26	bxc4	♖xc4
27	♖a1	♘f6
28	♖a3	♔c7
29	g3	h6
30	♔f1	a5

Chasing after the a4 pawn would have led to the exchange of rooks, which objectively is unfavourable for the defending side: 30...♘e4 31 ♔e1 ♘c3 32 ♖e3 ♘xa4 33 ♖f3 f6 34 ♖f4 (Tiviakov).

31	♔e1	♘e4
32	♖ee3!	g5
33	f3	♘d6
34	♔d1	♖c5
35	♔c1	h5
36	♖ac3	♖f5
37	♖ed3	♘c8
38	g4!	hxg4
39	fxg4	♖e5

After the opening of the position, the rooks have clearly 'come alive', and therefore it is important for Black to maintain a compact pawn mass. 39...♖f4 40 ♖f3 is unfavourable, while after 39...♖f1+ 40 ♔b2 ♘b6 again 41 ♖f3 is possible.

40	♖d4!	♘b6
41	♖h3	c5
42	♖d1	♖e4
43	♖f3	♖xg4

Weaker is 43...♘xa4 44 ♖xf7+ ♔c6 45 h3.

44	♖xf7+	♔c6
45	♖f6	♘xa4
46	♖xe6+	♔b5
47	♖d3	♖f4
48	♖g3	g4
49	♖e1!	

White cannot allow the activation of the rook after 49 ♖g6? ♖f1+ 50 ♔d2 ♖f2+ or 49 ♖e2 c4 50 ♖eg2 ♖f1+.

49	...	c4

Or 49...♖f2 50 ♖b3+ ♔c6 51 ♖e4.

50	♖eg1	♖f2
51	♖3g2	♖f3
52	♖xg4	♘c3
53	♖h1!	a4
54	h4	a3
55	h5	♖f2
56	♖gh4!	

Not forgetting about defence. After the careless 56 h6? ♘a2+ 57 ♔b1 ♘c3+ 58 ♔c1 White would have had to be content with a draw, but now in this variation he has gained the opportunity to play 58 ♔a1 (58...♖xc2 59 ♖4h2).

56...♖f7 57 h6 ♖h7 58 ♖g4 ♔c5 59 ♖g7 ♖h8 60 h7 a2 61 ♔b2 **Black resigns**

10 Main Line – Introduction

1	e4	e6
2	d4	d5
3	♘d2	c5
4	exd5	♛xd5
5	♘gf3	cxd4
6	♗c4	♛d6
7	0-0	♘f6
8	♘b3	♘c6
9	♘bxd4	♘xd4
10	♘xd4	

The main position in the 4...♛xd5 variation, and the critical one as regards evaluating this method of play against the Tarrasch Variation. White has a clear lead in development, and his spatial advantage is obvious. However, in view of Black's lack of pawn weaknesses, these advantages are of a temporary nature. Only, it is important for him to mobilise his pieces. But the insecure position of his queen (♘b5 is threatened) requires that he should first prepare a secure post for it.

This problem is solved by **10... ♗d7** (Chapters 11-13) or **10...a6** (Chapters 14-19).

The old continuation **10...♗e7** leads to a passive position, and therefore Black usually aims for the more active development of his bishop on the b8-h2 diagonal. After 11 b3 0-0 12 ♗b2 accurate play is required of Black:

(a) 12...e5 13 ♘b5 ♛xd1 14 ♖fxd1 ♗f5 15 ♖ac1 ♖fd8 16 ♗xe5!± (Tal-Uhlmann, Moscow 1967);

(b) 12...a6 13 ♛f3 ♛c7 14 ♖fe1 b5 15 ♗d3 ♗b7 16 ♛h3 g6 17 a4± (Stein-Uhlmann, Moscow 1968);

(c) 12...♛f4 13 ♛e2 ♗d7 (13... ♛e4? 14 ♛d2! ♖d8 15 ♖fe1 ♛h4

16 ♖ad1±, Geller-Vaganian, USSR Ch 1976 – *Game 18*) 14 ♖ad1 – 10...♗d7 11 b3 ♗e7.

<table>
<tr><td colspan="3">Game 18
Geller–Vaganian
USSR Championship 1976</td></tr>
</table>

1	e4	e6
2	d4	d5
3	♘d2	c5
4	♘gf3	cxd4
5	exd5	♕xd5
6	♗c4	♕d6
7	0-0	♘f6
8	♘b3	♘c6
9	♘bxd4	♘xd4
10	♘xd4	♗e7
11	b3	0-0
12	♗b2	♕f4
13	♕e2	♕e4?

At the time this game made such a strong impression that Black gave up playing 10...♗e7. This verdict would seem to be too severe, since the cause of Black's rapid defeat was this over-optimistic queen manoeuvre, which gave White an important tempo for the development of his rook.

13...♗d7 14 ♖ad1 would have led to a position from the game A.Sokolov-Smagin, examined under 10...♗d7 11 b3 ♗e7 (variation 13.31), in which Black achieved acceptable play.

14	♕d2!	♖d8
15	♖fe1	♕h4
16	♖ad1	♗c5

17	♖e5	

17 ♕a5 also looks strong, after which Black can defend his attacked pieces only by retreating his knight – 17...♘d7. Everything else loses: 17...b6 18 ♕xc5!; 17...♗b6 18 ♕xb6! or 17...♗e7 18 ♕xd8+! But the move played, surrounding the queen, is also unpleasant.

17	...	♘g4

Black stakes everything on a counterattack, since after 17...♗e7 he would have had to reckon with 18 g3.

18	♖xc5	♕xh2+
19	♔f1	e5
20	♕g5	♘f6
21	♗xf7+!	♔h8

If 21...♔xf7 White would have won by 22 ♖c7+ ♗d7 23 ♘f3.

22	♖xe5	♗g4
23	f3	♖ac8
24	♖d2	♖f8
25	♗e6	♖ce8

26 ♖de2 ♕h1 27 ♔f2 h5 28 ♘f5
Black resigns

11 10...♗d7 – Introduction

1	e4	e6
2	d4	d5
3	♘d2	c5
4	exd5	♕xd5
5	♘gf3	cxd4
6	♗c4	♕d6
7	0-0	♘f6
8	♘b3	♘c6
9	♘bxd4	♘xd4
10	♘xd4	♗d7

A logical developing move. Black takes control of b5 and demonstrates his readiness to castle queenside.

Now White's main continuations are **11 c3** (Chapter 12) and **11 b3** (Chapter 13).

Here we will consider:

11 ♗e3

White combines the defence of his knight with the development of his bishop, but at e3 the bishop becomes vulnerable to the standard attack by a knight, allowing Black to obtain a good game after castling on either side.

Other moves occur more rarely:

(a) 11 ♖e1 ♕c7 12 ♕e2 ♗c5 13 c3 ♗xd4 14 cxd4 ♖c8 15 b3 0-0 16 ♗g5 ♘d5= (A.Sokolov-Andersson, Tilburg 1987);

(b) 11 ♗b3 ♕c7 (11...♗e7 12 ♗g5 0-0 13 ♖e1 ♖fd8 14 c3 ♕c5 15 ♗h4 b5 16 a3 ♖ac8 17 ♕f3= ½-½, Ivanchuk-M.Gurevich, USSR Ch 1988) 12 ♕f3 0-0-0 13 ♗g5 ♕e5! (13...e5? 14 ♗xf6 gxf6 15 ♕xf6! ♖g8 16 ♘f5±, Watson-Rogers, Wijk aan Zee 1987 – *Game 19*) 14 ♕f4=;

(c) 11 a4 ♖c8 (11...♕c7 12 b3 – 11 b3 ♕c7 12 a4) 12 b3 ♕b8!?∞.

11	...	♕c7
12	♕e2	0-0-0

(a) 12...♘g4?! 13 ♕xg4 ♕xc4 14 ♖ad1 0-0-0 15 ♕g3! △ ♖d3;

(b) 12...♗d6 13 g3 0-0 14 ♘b5 ♗xb5 15 ♗xb5 ♘d5= (Armas-Touzane, France 1992).

13   a4

13 ♘b5 ♗xb5 14 ♗xb5 ♗c5∓.

13   ...   h5

14   h3

14 ♘b5? ♗xb5 15 axb5 ♘g4∓.

14   ...   ♗c5

15   c3!

15 b4 ♘g4! 16 hxg4 hxg4 17 f4 (17 g3? ♗xd4 18 ♗xd4 ♗c6∓∓) 17...gxf3 18 ♘xf3 (18 ♕xf3 ♕h2+ 19 ♔f2 ♗xd4 20 ♗xd4 ♗c6∓∓; 18 gxf3 ♗xd4 19 ♗xd4 ♖h4! 20 c3 ♖dh8∓∓) 18...♗xe3+ 19 ♕xe3 ♕xc4 20 ♘e5! (20 ♕xa7 ♖h5! △ ...♖dh8↑) 20...♕h4 21 ♕c5+ ♗c6= (Tal-Lobron, Marseille 1989).

15   ...   e5

16   ♘c2   ♗xe3

17   ♘xe3   ♗c6

18   ♖ad1   ♖xd1

19   ♖xd1   ♖d8

20   ♖xd8+   ♔xd8=

Game 19
Watson–Rogers
Wijk aan Zee 1987

---

1   e4   e6

2   d4   d5

3   ♘d2   c5

4   ♘gf3   cxd4

5   exd5   ♕xd5

6   ♗c4   ♕d6

7   0-0   ♘f6

8   ♘b3   ♘c6

9   ♘bxd4   ♘xd4

10   ♘xd4   ♗d7

11   ♗b3   ♕c7

12   ♕f3   0-0-0

13   ♗g5   e5?

A poor move, creating a whole complex of weaknesses. The strongest here is 13...♕e5!

14   ♗xf6   gxf6

15   ♕xf6!   ♖g8

16   ♘f5!

Black's idea would have been justified only after the co-operative 16 ♕xf7? ♗c5 17 ♘e6?! ♖xg2+! 18 ♔h1 ♖xf2!! 19 ♘xc7 ♖xf7 20 ♘d5 ♖xf1+ 21 ♖xf1 ♗c6 22 c4 b5! with a winning position (Rogers).

16   ...   ♗c5

17   ♖ad1   ♖df8

18   ♖fe1   ♖e8

19   ♘d6+?!

This allows Black to escape with the loss of just a pawn, whereas 19 ♗xf7 ♖ef8 20 ♖xe5 would have left him three pawns down.

19	...	♗xd6
20	♕xd6	♗c6
21	g3	♖e7
22	♕xc7+	♔xc7
23	♗d5	♖g6
24	c4	

24 f4 would have set Black more problems.

24	...	f5
25	b3	♖d6!
26	♗xc6	bxc6
27	♖xd6	♔xd6
28	♔f1?!	

White plays this ending too insipidly, allowing the enemy king into his rearguard. Black would have had more problems after 28 f4 e4 29 ♖d1+ ♔c5 30 ♔f2.

28	...	♔c5

29	♔e2	♔b4
30	♖d1	♔a3
31	♖d2	a5
32	♔e3	h5
33	h4	♖g7
34	♖d8	♔xa2
35	♖a8	f4+!
36	♔f3	

It is also a draw after 36 gxf4 exf4+ 37 ♔xf4 ♔xb3 38 ♖xa5 ♖g4+.

36	...	fxg3
37	fxg3	♔xb3
38	♖xa5	e4+
39	♔xe4	♖xg3
40	♖c5	♖g4+
41	♔d3	♖xh4
42	♖xc6	
		draw agreed

12   10...♗d7 11 c3

1	e4	e6
2	d4	d5
3	♘d2	c5
4	exd5	♕xd5
5	♘gf3	cxd4
6	♗c4	♕d6
7	0-0	♘f6
8	♘b3	♘c6
9	♘bxd4	♘xd4
10	♘xd4	♗d7
11	c3	

White defends his knight, in order to gain the possibility of developing his queen at e2 or f3. Black's main plans involve choosing between castling on the queenside with **11...0-0-0 (12.1)** or on the kingside after **11...♕c7 (12.2)**.

The less common 11...♗e7 also comes into consideration, for example:

(a) 12 ♕f3 ♖c8 13 ♗d3 ♕d5 14 ♕e2 0-0 15 ♖d1 ♖fd8= (Emms-Webster, British Ch 1992);

(b) 12 ♕e2 0-0 13 ♗g5 ♖ac8 14 ♗b3 ♖fe8 15 ♖fe1 ♕c5 16 ♗h4 ♘d5 17 ♗xe7 ♖xe7 18 ♖ad1 b5= (Mohr-Rahman, Moscow Olympiad 1994);

(c) 12 ♖e1 – see 9 ♖e1 ♗e7 10 ♘bxd4 ♘xd4 11 ♘xd4 0-0 12 c3 ♗d7 (section 8.21).

But more often Black prefers the more active development of his bishop at d6 after withdrawing his queen with 11...♕c7 (not fearing 12 ♕e2 ♗d6 13 ♘b5 ♗xb5 14 ♗xb5+ ♔e7, since the position of his king at e7 is perfectly secure). In combination with ....h7-h5 and ....♘g4 his attack may prove quite dangerous. The plan with queenside castling involves a certain degree of risk, in view of the open position of the king, and in recent times White's attack has more often been successful.

12.1

(1 e4 e6 2 d4 d5 3 ♘d2 c5 4 exd5 ♕xd5 5 ♘gf3 cxd4 6 ♗c4 ♕d6 7 0-0 ♘f6 8 ♘b3 ♘c6 9 ♘bxd4 ♘xd4 10 ♘xd4 ♗d7 11 c3)

11 ...   0-0-0

12   ♕e2
(a) 12 ♕f3 ♕c7 13 ♗b3 h5 14 h3 e5 15 ♘c2 e4= (Salazar-Klinger, Zurich 1985);
(b) 12 ♗e3 ♕c7 13 ♕e2 ♘g4 14 ♕xg4 ♕xc4= (Matanovic-Klinger, Vienna 1986);
(c) 12 ♖e1 ♕c7 13 ♕e2 h5 14 ♗g5 ♗d6 15 h3 ♗h2+ 16 ♔h1 ♗f4 17 ♗xf6 gxf6 18 ♗b5 ♕c5= (Kveinys-Glek, Bad Godesburg 1993).

12   ...   ♕c7
13   a4
13 ♗b5 ♗d6 14 ♗xd7+ ♖xd7 15 g3 a6= (Grünfeld-Maryasin, Israeli Ch 1992).
13   ...   h5
(a) 13...♘g4 14 g3 h5 15 h3 ♘e5 16 ♗f4 ♗d6 17 ♗xe5 ♗xe5 18 ♘b5 ♗xb5 19 axb5 h4 20 g4 ♗h2+?! (20...♔b8!?±) 21 ♔g2 ♕f4 22 ♖xa7± (Kudrin-Bonin, Philadelphia 1989);
(b) 13...♗d6 14 g3 h5 15 ♘b5 ♗xb5 16 axb5 b6 17 ♖a4!± (Adams-Djurhuus, Oakham 1992) – **Game 20**.

We now consider: **14 h3 (12.11)** and **14 ♘b5 (12.12)**.

12.11

(1 e4 e6 2 d4 d5 3 ♘d2 c5 4 exd5 ♕xd5 5 ♘gf3 cxd4 6 ♗c4 ♕d6 7 0-0 ♘f6 8 ♘b3 ♘c6 9 ♘bxd4 ♘xd4 10 ♘xd4 ♗d7 11 c3 0-0-0 12 ♕e2 ♕c7 13 a4 h5)

14   h3

14   ...   ♗c5
14...♗d6 15 ♘b5 ♗xb5 16 axb5 ♗c5 17 ♕f3 ♘g4 18 ♗f4 e5 19 ♗g3± (Emms-Bibby, British Ch 1990).
15   b4   ♗xd4
16   cxd4   ♔b8
16...♗c6 17 b5 ♗d5 18 ♗xd5 (18 ♗d3!? ♔b8 19 g3 ♔a8 20 a5→) 18...♖xd5 19 g3!± (Jansa-Marjanovic, Zenica 1986).
17   g3

17 b5 (17 ♗g5!?±) 17...♖c8 18 ♗d3 ♘d5 19 ♕f3± (Kosashvili-Djurhuus, Santiago 1990).

17	...	♔a8
18	♗f4	♕b6
19	a5	♕xd4
20	♖fd1	♕e4
21	♕xe4	♘xe4
22	♗c7±	

(Jansa).

12.12

(1 e4 e6 2 d4 d5 3 ♘d2 c5 4 exd5 ♕xd5 5 ♘gf3 cxd4 6 ♗c4 ♕d6 7 0-0 ♘f6 8 ♘b3 ♘c6 9 ♘bxd4 ♘xd4 10 ♘xd4 ♗d7 11 c3 0-0-0 12 ♕e2 ♕c7 13 a4 h5)

14 ♘b5

| 14 | ... | ♗xb5 |
| 15 | axb5 | ♗c5 |

15...♘g4 16 g3 ♗c5 17 ♔g2!± (Adams-Lautier, Biel 1991) – *Game 21*.

16 ♖a4!

16 b4 ♗b6 17 g3 ♘g4 18 ♔g2 ♕e5 19 h3 ♕f5! 20 hxg4 hxg4 21 ♗f4 g5∞ (Hellers-Djurhuus, Oslo 1991).

| 16 | ... | ♔b8 |

16...♘g4 17 g3!±.

| 17 | g3 | e5 |
| 18 | ♗e3!± | |

Pedersen-Djurhuus (Oslo 1992).

12.2

(1 e4 e6 2 d4 d5 3 ♘d2 c5 4 exd5 ♕xd5 5 ♘gf3 cxd4 6 ♗c4 ♕d6 7 0-0 ♘f6 8 ♘b3 ♘c6 9 ♘bxd4 ♘xd4 10 ♘xd4 ♗d7 11 c3)

| 11 | ... | ♕c7 |

12 ♕e2

12 ♗d3 0-0-0 (12...♗c5 13 ♗g5 ♗xd4 14 cxd4 ♗c6 15 b4, Krylov-Mamedova, Groningen 1994, 15...♘e4=) 13 ♕f3 ♗d6 14 h3 e5 15 ♘b5 ♗xb5 16 ♗xb5 e4 17 ♕e2 ♔b8 18 ♖e1 ♕c5∓ (Juarez-Celis, Buenos Aires 1993).

Now Black's main options are **12...♗d6 (12.21)** and **12...♗e7 (12.22)**. Alternatives:

(a) 12...0-0-0 – see section 12.1;

(b) 12...♗c5   13   ♗g5   0-0 (13...0-0-0!?±):

(b1) 14 ♖ad1 ♗d6? (14...♗e7 15 ♖fe1±) 15 ♗xf6 gxf6 16 ♕g4+ ♔h8 17 ♕h4!± (Jansa-Luther, Namestovo 1987) – *Game 22*;

(b2) 14 ♗xf6 gxf6 15 ♕g4+ ♔h8 16 ♕h4 ♕d8 17 ♖ad1± (Geenen-Goormachtigh, Belgian Ch 1990);

(c) 12...a6 13 ♗g5 ♗e7 14 ♖ad1 0-0 15 ♗d3= (W.Watson-Vaisser, Sochi 1988).

12.21

(1 e4 e6 2 d4 d5 3 ♘d2 c5 4 exd5 ♕xd5 5 ♘gf3 cxd4 6 ♗c4 ♕d6 7 0-0 ♘f6 8 ♘b3 ♘c6 9 ♘bxd4 ♘xd4 10 ♘xd4 ♗d7 11 c3 ♕c7 12 ♕e2)

12   ...   ♗d6

13   ♘b5

(a) 13 h3 ♗h2+ 14 ♔h1 ♗f4= (A.Sokolov-Ehlvest, USSR Ch 1988);

(b) 13 g3 0-0 14 ♗g5 ♖fc8 15 ♗d3 ♘d5 16 ♕e4 g6= (Lautier-Andersson, Clermont-Ferrand 1989).

13   ...   ♗xb5
14   ♗xb5+   ♔e7
15   g3   a6

(a) 15...h5?!:

(a1) 16 ♗g5 h4 17 ♖ad1 hxg3 18 hxg3 ♕c5 19 ♗e3 ♕f5 20 ♖fe1 ♖ad8 21 ♗xa7 ♖h5∞ (Collinson-Bus, Oakham 1992);

(a2) 16 h4!? ♘g4 (16...♖ac8 17 ♗g5±) 17 ♔g2 a6 18 ♗a4 ♖hc8 19 ♗g5+! ♔f8 20 ♖ad1± (Psakhis-Herzog, Vienna 1991);

(b) 15...♖hd8 16 ♖e1 ♖ac8 (16...h6 17 ♕f3±, Jansa-Smagin, Trnava 1987) 17 ♕f3 a6 18 ♗f1± (A.Sokolov-Andersson, Clermont-Ferrand 1989);

(c) 15...a5 16 ♕f3 ♖hd8 17 ♖d1 ♕b6!? 18 a4 ♗c5 19 ♗d2 ♖d5 20 ♗e1 ♖ad8= (Ye Jiangchuan-Hug, Biel Interzonal 1991).

16   ♗a4

16 ♗d3!? △ ♕f3, ♖d1, ♗f1-g2± (Ivanchuk).

16   ...   ♖hd8
17   ♕f3   h6
18   ♗b3

18 ♗e3 ♖ac8 19 ♗d4 b5 (19...e5? 20 ♗e3 e4 21 ♕e2 ♔f8 22 ♖ad1 ♗e5 23 ♗b3!±, Rozentalis-Djurhuus, Oslo 1992) 20 ♗b3 ♗c5! 21 ♗xc5+ ♕xc5 22 a4 ♖d2!= (Djurhuus).

18 ... ♖ab8
19 ♖d1±

Ivanchuk-Ehlvest (Manila Olympiad 1992) – *Game 23*.

12.22

(1 e4 e6 2 d4 d5 3 ♘d2 c5 4 exd5 ♕xd5 5 ♘gf3 cxd4 6 ♗c4 ♕d6 7 0-0 ♘f6 8 ♘b3 ♘c6 9 ♘bxd4 ♘xd4 10 ♘xd4 ♗d7 11 c3 ♕c7 12 ♕e2)

12 ... ♗e7

13 ♗g5 0-0
14 ♖ad1

(a) 14 ♖fe1 ♘d5 15 ♗xe7 ♘xe7 16 ♗d3 ♘d5 17 ♕e4 ♘f6 18 ♕h4 h6 19 ♘f3 ♖fd8= (Korolev-Rubinchik, corr. 1988);

(b) 14 ♗b3 ♘d5 15 ♗xe7 ♘xe7 16 ♖ad1 ♘g6 17 g3 ♖ad8= (Hracek-Glek, Stare Mesto 1992).

14 ... ♖fe8

14...♘d5 15 ♗xe7 ♘xe7 16 ♘xe6!? ♗xe6 17 ♗xe6 fxe6 18

♕xe6+ ♖f7 19 ♖d7 ♕c5 20 ♖xb7⩲↑.

15 ♗h4 ♘d5
16 ♗xe7

16 ♗g3 ♘f4= (Blatny-Glek, Stare Mesto 1992).

16 ... ♘xe7
17 ♖d2 ♘g6
18 ♖fd1 ♘f4
19 ♕f1 ♖ad8
20 ♗b5 ♕b6
21 a4 e5=

Rozentalis-Glek (Germany 1992).

Game 20
Adams–Djurhuus
Oakham 1992

1 e4 e6
2 d4 d5
3 ♘d2 c5
4 exd5 ♕xd5
5 ♘gf3 cxd4
6 ♗c4 ♕d6
7 0-0 ♘f6
8 ♘b3 ♘c6
9 ♘bxd4 ♘xd4
10 ♘xd4 ♗d7
11 c3 ♕c7
12 ♕e2 0-0-0
13 a4 ♗d6
14 g3!

After 14 h3 Black maintains the balance by a standard manoeuvre in this type of position – 14...♗h2+ 15 ♔h1 ♗f4.

14 ... h5
15 ♘b5 ♗xb5
16 axb5

16 ...   b6

The queenside pawn structure in the diagram position is typical for the plan with queenside castling, and is rather unpleasant for Black, who is nevertheless forced to weaken his king's position. Is this not a reason for him to give preference to 10...a6? Here it is too late for him to stake everything with 16...h4 17 ♖xa7 hxg3 18 ♖a8+ ♔d7 19 ♖xd8+ ♔xd8 20 hxg3.

17 ♖a4!   ♔b8?

In positions with castling on opposite sides every tempo is important. Black should have played 17...h4, and only if 18 ♕f3 ♔b8. Now he gets a worse version of this.

18 ♗g5!   h4
19 ♗xh4

Not giving Black any illusions such as 19 ♖fa1 hxg3 20 ♖xa7 (20 hxg3 ♕b7!) 20...♕c5, and 19...♖xh4 20 gxh4 ♗xh2+ is pointless on account of 21 ♔g2.

19	...	♕c5
20	♗xf6	gxf6
21	♖fa1	♖d7
22	♕f3	♖h5

If 22...♕h5 the queen's place is taken by the bishop: 23 ♕xh5 ♖xh5 24 ♗e2! ♖e5 25 ♗f3.

23	♗d3	♕d5
24	♗e4	♕e5
25	♗c6	♖c7
26	♖d4	♖h8
27	b4	♗e7
28	♕d3	f5?
29	♗g2!	

Black resigns

Game 21
Adams–Lautier
Biel 1991

1	e4	e6
2	d4	d5
3	♘d2	c5
4	exd5	♕xd5
5	♘gf3	cxd4
6	♗c4	♕d6
7	0-0	♘f6
8	♘b3	♘c6
9	♘bxd4	♘xd4
10	♘xd4	♗d7
11	c3	♕c7
12	♕e2	0-0-0
13	a4	h5
14	♘b5	♗xb5
15	axb5	♘g4

The immediate 15...♗c5 is considered more accurate, but after 16 ♖a4! things are no easier for Black.

| 16 | g3 | ♗c5 |

17	♔g2!	♔b8
18	♖a4	

Compared with the previous game Black has made greater progress: his pieces are more active, and his king's position has not been weakened. But the threat of a pawn offensive still gives him defensive problems. Here 18...e5 followed by ....f7-f5 and ...h5-h4 suggests itself, since 19 h3 ♘f6 20 ♗g5 (20 ♗e3 Δ ♖fa1 – Adams) 20...h4! 21 ♗xh4 ♖xh4! 22 gxh4 e4 or 19 ♗e3!? ♘xe3+ 20 fxe3 f6 gives Black counterplay.

18	...	♖he8?
19	h3	♘f6
20	♗g5	♖d7
21	♖fa1	♘d5

This allows White to win the a7 pawn, but what else is there?

22	♗xd5!	♖xd5
23	♗f4	e5
24	b4	♕d7
25	♗g5	♗b6
26	c4	♖d3

27	c5	♕xb5

In the hope of 28 cxb6? ♖xg3+ 29 ♔f1 ♖g1+, but...

28	♔h2!	♗c7
29	♖xa7	♔c8
30	♖a8+	♗b8
31	♖d1	

Black resigns

Game 22
Jansa–Luther
Namestovo 1987

1	e4	e6
2	d4	d5
3	♘d2	c5
4	♘gf3	cxd4
5	exd5	♕xd5
6	♗c4	♕d6
7	0-0	♘f6
8	♘b3	♘c6
9	♘bxd4	♘xd4
10	♘xd4	♗d7
11	c3	♕c7
12	♕e2	♗c5
13	♗g5	0-0
14	♖ad1	

14 ...   &d6?

Too optimistic. 14...&e7 was essential.

15	&xf6	gxf6
16	♕g4+	♔h8
17	♕h4!	♕xc4
18	♕xf6+	♔g8
19	♕g5+	♔h8
20	♕f6+	♔g8
21	♖fe1!	♖fd8

After 21...&c6 22 ♘xc6 ♕xc6 the other rook joins the attack by 23 ♖d4.

| 22 | ♖e4 | ♕d5 |

After 22...e5 23 ♘f5 the queen is lost.

| 23 | ♖g4+ | ♔f8 |
| 24 | ♖g5! | ♕e4 |

If 24...e5 White wins by 25 c4! ♕c5 26 ♖g7.

25	♕h6+	♔e7
26	♘f5+	♕xf5
27	♖xf5	

Black resigns

Game 23
Ivanchuk–Ehlvest
Manila Olympiad 1992

1	e4	e6
2	d4	d5
3	♘d2	c5
4	exd5	♕xd5
5	♘gf3	cxd4
6	&c4	♕d6
7	0-0	♘f6
8	♘b3	♘c6
9	♘bxd4	♘xd4
10	♘xd4	&d7
11	c3	♕c7

12	♕e2	&d6
13	♘b5	&xb5
14	&xb5+	♔e7
15	g3	a6

Black immediately drives away the bishop. He can also consider the plan with 15...a5 16 ♕f3 ♖hd8 17 ♖d1 ♕b6 18 a4 &c5.

16	&a4	♖hd8
17	♕f3	h6
18	&b3	♖ab8
19	♖d1	a5
20	a4	♕c6
21	♔g2	

After the exchange of queens White has no more than equality. As a try for an advantage, Ivanchuk recommends 21 ♕e2 &c5 22 &f4.

21	...	♘d7!
22	&c2	♘e5
23	♕xc6	bxc6!
24	♖b1	♘c4
25	♔f3	

It is more accurate to drive away the knight with 25 b3 ♘b6 26 c4.

25	...	♘b6
26	♔e2	♖b7
27	♖d4?!	

Not allowing the knight in at c4, but here the rook becomes vulnerable. White could have achieved the same aim with 27 b3 ♘d5 28 &d2, at the same time reminding Black of his weakness at a5.

| 27 | ... | ♖db8 |
| 28 | &e4 | &e5 |

By playing 28...&c5! 29 &xc6 ♖c7 30 &f4 ♖xc6 31 &xb8 &xd4 32 cxd4 ♘xa4 Black could have seized the initiative (Ivanchuk).

29 ♗xc6 ♗xd4?!

And now 29...♖c7, when 30 ♖e4 ♖xc6 31 ♖xe5 ♘xa4 32 ♗d2 is merely good enough to maintain equality.

30 ♗xb7 ♖xb7
31 cxd4 ♘xa4
32 ♖a1

32 ... ♖b4?

Here the rook is clearly overloaded. It was more natural to centralise the knight by 32...♘b6 33 ♖xa5 ♘d5.

33 ♗d2 ♖xd4
34 ♗e3?!

After 34 b4! White would have created a dangerous passed pawn.

34 ... ♖b4
35 b3 ♘c3+
36 ♔d3 ♘d5?

The exchange down, Black cannot hope for a draw, whereas 36...♘e4 37 ♖xa5 f5 would have left him with chances of a successful defence.

37 ♗c5+ ♔f6
38 ♗xb4 axb4
39 h4 g5
40 h5 g4
41 ♖a7 ♘c3
42 ♖b7
Black resigns

13   10...♗d7 11 b3

1	e4	e6
2	d4	d5
3	♘d2	c5
4	exd5	♕xd5
5	♘gf3	cxd4
6	♗c4	♕d6
7	0-0	♘f6
8	♘b3	♘c6
9	♘bxd4	♘xd4
10	♘xd4	♗d7
11	b3	

White defends his light-square bishop and prepares to fianchetto his dark-square bishop. On the long diagonal it will be aimed at the kingside and will control the important e5 square, where he may be able to establish his knight. A drawback to the fianchetto is that the f4 square is no longer controlled, and so often Black aims to keep his king on the queenside and to use his dark-square bishop on the b8-h2 diagonal for an attack on the kingside. This aim is pursued by the main plans **11...a6 (13.1)** and **11... 0-0-0 (13.2)**, but the plan with kingside castling after **11...♗e7 (13.3)** is also possible.

The immediate 11...♕c7?! is premature on account of 12 ♘b5! (there is also 12 a4 ♗d6 13 ♘b5 ♗xb5 14 ♗xb5+ ♔e7 15 g3 ♖hd8 16 ♕f3 ♖ac8 17 ♗b2±, Mrva-Bus, Odessa 1990) 12...♕e5 13 ♕e1! ♕xe1 14 ♖xe1 ♗xb5 15 ♗xb5+± (Tiviakov-Keitlinghaus, Groningen 1991).

11...h5?! is strongly met by 12 ♘b5! ♕e5 13 ♕e1! (13 ♕f3? ♗xb5 14 ♕xb7 ♖b8∓∓) 13...♕xa1 (13...♕b4 14 g3 Δ ♗f4±) 14 ♘c7+ ♔d8 15 ♘xa8 ♗d6 16 ♕a5+ ♔e7 17 c3 b6 18 ♕xa7 b5 19 ♗a3 ♕xc3 (Miles-Nenashev, Agios Nikolaos 1995) 20 ♗xd6+±± (Miles).

13.1

(1 e4 e6 2 d4 d5 3 ♘d2 c5 4 exd5 ♕xd5 5 ♘gf3 cxd4 6 ♗c4 ♕d6 7 0-0 ♘f6 8 ♘b3 ♘c6 9 ♘bxd4 ♘xd4 10 ♘xd4 ♗d7 11 b3)

11 ... a6

This position is often reached via the move order 10...a6 11 b3 ♗d7.

12 ♗b2 ♕c7

(a) 12...♗e7 13 ♕e2 0-0 14
♖fd1! (14 ♖ad1 ♕c5 15 a4 ♖ad8 16
♘f3±, Popovic-Short, Dubai Olympiad 1986) 14...♕c5 15 a4±
(Popovic);

(b) 12...♕f4 13 ♕e2 ♗d6 14 g3
♕g4 15 ♕xg4 ♘xg4 16 ♖ad1 ♗c5
17 ♘f3!? (17 ♗e2 e5!±, Ernst-Rogers, Lugano 1989 – *Game 24*)
17...f6 18 h3 ♘h6±;

(c) 12...b5 13 ♗d3 ♗e7 14 ♕e2
0-0 15 ♖ad1 ♕c5! (15...♖fd8? 16
♘xb5! axb5 17 ♗xf6 ♕b4 18 ♗xe7
♕xe7 19 ♗xb5±, Istratescu-Cosma,
Bucharest 1994) 16 ♘f3 ♗c6 17
♘e5 ♗b7 18 c4! bxc4 19 ♗xc4±
(Istratescu).

13 ♕e2   0-0-0
13...♗d6 14 ♘f5 (14 h3 0-0 15
♖ad1 ♖ad8, Yudasin-Ehlvest, USSR
Ch 1988, 16 ♗d3±) 14... 0-0-0 15
♘xg7 ♘d5 16 ♗xd5 exd5 17 ♕h5±
(Tiviakov-Smyslov, Rostov 1993).
14 ♘f3
14 ♖ad1 ♗d6 15 h3 ♖he8
(15...h5?! 16 ♘f3! ♗c6 17 ♘e5±,

Luecke-Luther, Borsodtavho 1991)
16 a4 h6 17 ♖fe1 e5 18 ♘f3 e4 19
♘d4 e3 20 fxe3 ♗h2+ 21 ♔h1 ♘e4
22 ♕f3 ♘g5 23 ♕f1 ♘e4 ½-½
(Ernst-Johannesson, Gausdal 1995).
14 ...   ♗d6
(a) 14...h5 15 ♖ad1 ♗c5 16 ♗e5
♕c6 17 h3 ♘e8 (Psakhis-Nikolic,
Sochi 1992) 18 ♗g3 f6 19 b4!→;

(b) 14...♗c6 15 ♘e5 ♔b8 16
♕e3!± (Tiviakov-Degerman, Gausdal 1993) – *Game 25*.
15 ♘e5   ♗e8
16 ♖ad1±

13.2

(1 e4 e6 2 d4 d5 3 ♘d2 c5 4 exd5
♕xd5 5 ♘gf3 cxd4 6 ♗c4 ♕d6 7
0-0 ♘f6 8 ♘b3 ♘c6 9 ♘bxd4
♘xd4 10 ♘xd4 ♗d7 11 b3)

11 ...   0-0-0

12 ♗b2
12 a4!?:
(a) 12...♕c7 13 ♕e2 a6
(13...♗c5 14 ♘b5 ♗xb5 15 axb5 h5

16 ♗b2 ♘g4 17 g3 ♖h6 18 ♖a4±, Ljubojevic-Lobron, Reggio Emilia 1985/6) 14 b4 ♘g4 (14...♗xb4 15 ♗xa6!→) 15 g3 e5 16 ♘b5!±→ (Mann-Charpentier, corr. 1992/3) – *Game 26*;

(b) 12...h5!? 13 ♗b2 ♕f4 (13... ♕c7 14 ♕e2 ♘g4∞) 14 g3 ♕g4=.

12 ...   ♕c7
13 ♕e2   h5

13...♗d6 14 h3 a6 15 ♖ad1 h5 16 ♘f3! ♗c6 17 ♘e5± (Frolov-Naumkin, Alushta 1992).

14 ♘f3

(a) 14 ♖fd1? ♘g4 15 g3 ♗c5 16 ♖f1 e5∓→ (Nenashev-Naumkin, Moscow 1985);

(b) 14 h3?! ♘g4! 15 f4 (15 hxg4 hxg4 16 f4 gxf3 17 ♘xf3 ♗c6 18 ♘e5 ♗c5+ 19 ♖f2 ♖h4 Δ 20... ♖dh8∓) 15...♘h6 16 ♕xh5 ♗c5 17 ♕e5 ♘f5∓ (Grünfeld-Lobron, New York 1985);

(c) 14 a4 ♘g4 15 g3 a6 (15...♘xh2!?) 16 ♘b5 axb5 17 axb5 ♔b8 18 ♖a4 ♗c5 19 b4 ♗b6 20 ♗d3? (20 ♗b3!?∞) 20...♗c8 21 c4 ♕d6∓ (Geller-Naumkin, Palma de Mallorca 1989).

14 ...   ♘g4

14...♗c6 15 ♘e5 ♘g4 16 ♖ad1! (16 h3?! ♗a3!∓, Dvoiris-Dokhoyan, Aktyubinsk 1985) 16...♖xd1 (16... ♗d6 17 ♘xf7!±±) 17 ♖xd1± (Dvoiris-Eingorn, Kharkov 1985).

15 h3 (13.21)
15 ♖ad1 (13.22)

15 ♗e5 ♘xe5 16 ♘xe5 ♗e8 17 f4 ♗d6 18 ♖ae1 ♔b8 Δ ...f7-f6∓ (Zso.Polgar-Peng, Thessaloniki Olympiad 1988).

13.21

(1 e4 e6 2 d4 d5 3 ♘d2 c5 4 exd5 ♕xd5 5 ♘gf3 cxd4 6 ♗c4 ♕d6 7 0-0 ♘f6 8 ♘b3 ♘c6 9 ♘bxd4 ♘xd4 10 ♘xd4 ♗d7 11 b3 0-0-0 12 ♗b2 ♕c7 13 ♕e2 h5 14 ♘f3 ♘g4)

15 h3   ♗c6

16 ♖fd1
16 ♘e5 ♘xe5 17 ♗xe5 ♗d6 18 ♗xd6 ♕xd6 19 ♖ad1 ♕c5 (Geller-Arkhipov, USSR 1988).

16 ... ♗c5
16...♗d6? 17 hxg4 hxg4 18 ♘e5 ♖h5 19 ♘xf7!±± (Ernst-Lutz, Berlin 1986).

17 ♖xd8+ ♕xd8
18 hxg4
18 ♖f1 ♖h6!→ (Matulovic-Marjanovic, Yugoslavia 1986).

18 ... hxg4
19 ♗xe6+ fxe6
20 ♕xe6+ ♗d7 21 ♕c4 gxf3 22 ♕xc5+∞ (Lanka-Glek, USSR 1989) – *Game 27*.

13.22

(1 e4 e6 2 d4 d5 3 ♘d2 c5 4 exd5 ♕xd5 5 ♘gf3 cxd4 6 ♗c4 ♕d6 7 0-0 ♘f6 8 ♘b3 ♘c6 9 ♘bxd4 ♘xd4 10 ♘xd4 ♗d7 11 b3 0-0-0 12 ♗b2 ♕c7 13 ♕e2 h5 14 ♘f3 ♘g4)

15 ♖ad1

15 ... ♗d6
15...♗c5?! 16 h3 ♗c6 17 ♖xd8+ ♕xd8 18 ♗xe6+!± (Yandemirov-Glek, Podolsk 1990).

16 h3 ♗c6
17 ♖fe1
17 ♖xd6? ♕xd6 18 hxg4 hxg4 19 ♘e5 ♖h4 20 ♘xg4 ♖dh8 21 f3 ♕g3∓∓ (Tseshkovsky-Glek, Philadelphia 1990).

17 ... ♗c5
18 ♖xd8+ ♕xd8
19 ♗xe6+! fxe6
20 ♕xe6+ ♔b8
21 hxg4 hxg4
21...♖e8? 22 ♕c4± (Yandemirov-Vainerman, Lvov 1986).

22 ♗e5+ ♔a8
23 ♕xg4 ♗xf3∞
(Glek).

13.3

(1 e4 e6 2 d4 d5 3 ♘d2 c5 4 exd5 ♕xd5 5 ♘gf3 cxd4 6 ♗c4 ♕d6 7 0-0 ♘f6 8 ♘b3 ♘c6 9 ♘bxd4 ♘xd4 10 ♘xd4 ♗d7 11 b3)

11 ... ♗e7

12 ♗b2 (13.31)
12 a4 (13.32)

13.31

(1 e4 e6 2 d4 d5 3 ♘d2 c5 4 exd5 ♕xd5 5 ♘gf3 cxd4 6 ♗c4 ♕d6 7 0-0 ♘f6 8 ♘b3 ♘c6 9 ♘bxd4 ♘xd4 10 ♘xd4 ♗d7 11 b3 ♗e7)

12 ♗b2 0-0
13 ♕e2

(a) 13 ♖e1 ♖fe8 14 ♘f3 ♕xd1 15 ♖axd1 ♖ed8 16 ♘e5 ♗e8= (Liberzon-Spassky, Baden 1980);

(b) 13 ♕f3!? ♕c7 14 ♖fe1 ♖fe8 15 ♘b5±.

13 ... ♕f4

(a) 13...a6? 14 ♘f5! exf5 15 ♖ad1±;

(b) 13...♖fe8 14 ♖ad1 ♕b6 15 ♘f3 ♖ad8= (Khalifman-Kholmov, Minsk 1985).

14 ♖ad1 ♖fd8
15 ♖fe1

15 ♖d3?! e5! 16 ♖e1 (16 ♖f3 ♗g4 17 ♗xf7+ ♔h8∓) 16...e4∓.

15 ... ♗b4
16 c3 ♗d6
17 g3 ♕g4
18 ♕xg4

18 ♕f1?! e5!∓ (A.Sokolov-Smagin, USSR Ch 1985) – *Game 28*.

18 ... ♘xg4=

(1 e4 e6 2 d4 d5 3 ♘d2 c5 4 exd5 ♕xd5 5 ♘gf3 cxd4 6 ♗c4 ♕d6 7 0-0 ♘f6 8 ♘b3 ♘c6 9 ♘bxd4 ♘xd4 10 ♘xd4 ♗d7 11 b3 ♗e7)

12 a4

12 ... a6
13 ♖e1

13 ♗b2!?±.

13 ... ♕c7

13...♖d8 14 ♗b2 ♗c8 15 ♕e2 ♕c5 (15...0-0 16 ♘f5±) 16 ♘f3 0-0 17 ♘e5± (Tiviakov-Kholmov, Moscow 1992).

14 ♕f3

14 ♗b2 0-0-0±.

14 ... 0-0

14...0-0-0 15 ♘f5!? ♗b4 (15... ♗c6 16 ♕g3) 16 ♗f4 ♕c6 17 ♕c3!!± (Tiviakov).

15 ♘f5

15 ♗f4 ♗d6 16 ♗xd6 ♕xd6 17 ♖ad1±.

15 ... ♗d8
16 ♘xg7 ♔xg7

17   ♗b2   ♖g8!±
Tiviakov-Andersson (Haninge 1992) – *Game 29*.

Game 24
Ernst–Rogers
Lugano 1989

1	e4	e6
2	d4	d5
3	♘d2	c5
4	exd5	♕xd5
5	♘gf3	cxd4
6	♗c4	♕d6
7	0-0	♘f6
8	♘b3	♘c6
9	♘bxd4	♘xd4
10	♘xd4	♗d7
11	b3	a6
12	♗b2	♕f4!?

A clever regrouping idea. The usual post for the queen is at c7.

13   ♕e2
13 ♘f3 ♗c6 14 ♘e5 ♖d8 is unclear, but perhaps simplest is the immediate 13 g3.

13   ...   ♗d6!
14   g3
Now on 14 ♘f3?! ♗c6 15 ♘e5 Black has 15...♘d7! 16 g3 ♘xe5 with equality.

14   ...   ♕g4
15   ♕xg4
Otherwise 15 f3 ♕h3.

15   ...   ♘xg4
16   ♖ad1   ♗c5
17   ♗e2
It would have been stronger to prevent Black's next move – 17

♘f3!, with the more pleasant ending.

17   ...   e5!
18   ♘f3   e4
18...f6 19 ♘d2 ♗f5! is also good.

19   ♘g5
This allows a tactical stroke by Black, but 19 ♘e5 ♗xe5 20 ♗xe5 f6 leads only to equality.

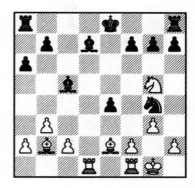

19   ...   ♘e3!
20   ♖xd7?!
Rogers considers the best to be 20 fxe3 ♗xe3+ 21 ♔g2 ♗xg5 22 ♗xg7 ♖g8 23 ♗f6, retaining the initiative.

20   ...   ♔xd7
21   ♖e1   f5!
22   ♘f7   ♖hc8!
Not allowing White to consolidate his forces, which he would easily have done after 22...♘g4?! 23 ♗xg4 fxg4 24 ♘xh8 ♖xh8 25 ♖xe4, with advantage.

23   fxe3   ♗xe3+
24   ♔f1   ♖xc2
25   ♘e5+   ♔e7

| 26 | ♘c4 | ♝c5 |
| 27 | ♝xg7?! | |

White regretted this after Black's reply. It would have been better to exchange the active rook (27 ♖c1), which is destined to run amok.

| 27 | ... | f4! |
| 28 | ♝h6 | |

Of course, not 28 gxf4 ♖g8.

28	...	f3
29	♝d1	♖f2+
30	♔g1	♖e2+
31	♔f1	♖f2+
32	♔g1	♖xa2+
33	♔h1	♔f6!
34	♖xe4	♖a1
35	♖e1	♖d8
36	♝d2	♝b4!
37	♝xf3	♖xe1+
38	♝xe1	♝xe1
39	♝xb7	a5

Now the endgame is purely a matter of technique.

40	♝c6	♖d3
41	♝a4	♖f3!
42	♔g1	♔e6
43	♔g2	♖f2+
44	♔h3	♝c3

45 ♝c6 ♖a2 46 ♝e4 h6 47 ♝c6 ♔f5 48 ♘e3+ ♔g5 49 ♘g2 ♖b2 50 ♝d5 ♔f6! 51 ♘h4 ♔e5 52 ♝g8 ♔e4! 53 ♝h7+ ♔d5 54 ♝g8+ ♔c5 55 ♘g6 ♔b4 56 ♘e7 ♔a3 57 ♘c6 ♖d2 58 ♝c4 ♖d6 59 ♘a7 ♔b4 60 ♝g8 ♖g6 61 ♝d5 ♖d6 62 ♝g8 ♝d4 63 ♘c8 ♖d8 64 ♝e6 ♝c5! 65 ♔g4 ♖d3 66 ♔h5 ♖xb3 67 ♔xh6 a4 68 g4 a3 69 g5 a2 70 g6 ♝d4 **White resigns**

1	e4	e6
2	d4	d5
3	♘d2	c5
4	exd5	♕xd5
5	♘gf3	cxd4
6	♝c4	♕d6
7	0-0	♘f6
8	♘b3	♘c6
9	♘bxd4	♘xd4
10	♘xd4	a6
11	b3	♝d7

A position from the 10...♝d7 11 b3 variation has been reached by transposition.

12	♝b2	♕c7
13	♕e2	0-0-0
14	♘f3	♝c6

14...♝d6 15 ♘e5 ♝e8 is sounder.

| 15 | ♘e5 | |

| 15 | ... | ♔b8 |

The situation is not eased by 15...♗d5 or 15...♘d5, since after 16 ♗xd5 any piece recapture is answered by 17 c4, retaining control over the important central squares.

16   ♕e3!

Probing the weak b6 square (16...♗d5 17 ♗d4).

16   ...   ♘d5
17   ♗xd5   ♗xd5?!

After 17...exd5 Tiviakov would still have retained the advantage by 18 c4 f6 19 ♘xc6+ ♕xc6 20 ♖ad1, but even so this was better.

18   c4   ♗c5?!
19   ♕g3   f6
20   cxd5   ♗d6
21   ♖ac1   ♕e7
22   dxe6   ♕xe6

Black also loses after 22...fxe5 23 ♖cd1 ♕xe6 24 ♖xd6.

23   ♕g4

Black resigns

Game 26
Mann-Charpentier
Correspondence 1992/3

1	e4	e6
2	d4	d5
3	♘d2	c5
4	♘gf3	cxd4
5	exd5	♕xd5
6	♗c4	♕d6
7	0-0	♘f6
8	♘b3	♘c6
9	♘bxd4	♘xd4
10	♘xd4	♗d7
11	b3	0-0-0
12	a4	♕c7

13   ♕e2   a6

13...♗c5 also has its problems, since it allows White to open the a-file for his attack – 14 ♘b5 ♗xb5 15 axb5 etc.

14   b4   ♘g4
15   g3   e5

16   ♘b5!

A spectacular move. White emphasises the insecure position of the black king, not begrudging his knight for the sake of opening the a-file. Black evidently cannot decline the sacrifice with 16...♕b8, since after 17 h3 ♘f6 18 ♗e3 his defensive problems increase.

16   ...   axb5
17   axb5   ♕b6

17...♔b8 is also an unreliable defence. After 18 c3 White is threatening to play his queen to a2, and all the same the c7 square has to be vacated.

18   c3   ♗d6

After 18...♗e6 White would have intensified the threats by 19

♖a8+ ♔c7 20 ♗xe6 ♕xe6 21 b6+ ♔d7 22 ♕e4.

19   h3   f5

19...h5 20 hxg4 ♗xg4 21 ♕a2 h4 22 ♗e3 ♕c7 23 ♗xf7 hxg3 24 ♗e6+ is also insufficient (Bottlik).

20   hxg4   f4
21   gxf4   exf4
22   ♗e6   ♔b8

22...♖hf8 23 ♖a8+ ♗b8 is a tougher defence, although even then after 24 ♗xd7+ ♖xd7 25 c4 White, apart from his two extra pawns, also retains an attack (for example, he is threatening to play his bishop to e5).

23   ♗xd7   ♖xd7
24   c4   ♗xb4
25   ♗xf4+   ♗d6
26   c5!   ♕xc5
27   ♖fc1
       Black resigns

Game 27
Lanka–Glek
Moscow 1989

1	e4	e6
2	d4	d5
3	♘d2	c5
4	♘gf3	cxd4
5	exd5	♕xd5
6	♗c4	♕d6
7	0-0	♘f6
8	♘b3	♘c6
9	♘bxd4	♘xd4
10	♘xd4	♗d7
11	b3	0-0-0
12	♗b2	♕c7

13   ♕e2   h5
14   ♘f3   ♘g4
15   h3

The other main continuation is 15 ♖ad1 ♗d6.

15   ...   ♗c6
16   ♖fd1

16   ...   ♗c5

In this variation the black pieces are developed in the most active positions possible. To avoid the worst White forces exchanges.

17   ♖xd8+   ♕xd8
18   hxg4   hxg4
19   ♗xe6+   fxe6
20   ♕xe6+   ♗d7

20...♔b8 is also possible, practically forcing White to confine himself to 21 ♕xg4 ♗xf3! 22 ♕xf3 (22 gxf3 ♗xf2+!) 22...♖f8! with roughly equal chances, since it is risky to play 21 ♕e5+?! ♔a8! 22 ♕xc5 gxf3 23 ♗xg7 (or 23 ♗d4 ♕b8 24 g3 ♖h3!) 23...fxg2! 24 f3 ♖h1+ 25 ♔xg2 ♕d2+! 26 ♔g3 ♕h2+, when Black wins (Glek).

21	♕c4	gxf3
22	♕xc5+	♗c6
23	♕d4?	

Now the pawn advances to g2 where it paralyses White's forces in the endgame. It was essential to play 23 ♕f5+! ♕d7 (if 23...♚b8 White can capture 24 ♗xg7) 24 ♕xd7+ ♚xd7 25 g3.

23	...	♕xd4
24	♗xd4	fxg2
25	f3	♗xf3
26	♗xg7	♖h1+
27	♚f2	♚d7
28	♖g1?	

A significant loss of time. It was essential to take immediate control of g1 with the bishop (28 ♗d4).

28	...	♗e4
29	♗d4	a6
30	c3	♚e6
31	a4	♚f5
32	b4	♖h3!
33	b5	a5
34	♖e1	♖d3!
35	♚g1	♖d2
36	♖a1	♚g4!
37	♗b6	♖d6!
38	♗xa5	♖h6
39	♚f2	♖f6+
40	♚g1	♖h6
41	♚f2	b6!
42	♖e1	

After 42 ♗b4 the king decides matters: 42...♖f6+ 43 ♚g1 ♚f3 44 ♖a2 ♚g3.

42	...	♖f6+
43	♚g1	♚f3!

White resigns

Game 28
A.Sokolov–Smagin
USSR Championship 1985

1	e4	e6
2	d4	d5
3	♘d2	c5
4	♘gf3	cxd4
5	exd5	♕xd5
6	♗c4	♕d6
7	0-0	♘f6
8	♘b3	♘c6
9	♘bxd4	♘xd4
10	♘xd4	♗d7
11	b3	♗e7
12	♗b2	0-0

To some extent this game rehabilitates the reputation of the 10...♗e7 11 b3 0-0 12 ♗b2 variation, which was practically shelved in the 1960s.

13	♕e2	♕f4!?
14	♖ad1	♖fd8
15	♖fe1	♗b4
16	c3	♗d6
17	g3	♕g4
18	♕f1?!	

White is too optimistic, otherwise he would have exchanged queens.

18	...	e5!
19	♗e2	♕g6
20	♘b5	♗c5
21	♗a3	♗b6
22	♘d6	♘g4
23	♗xg4	♗xg4
24	♖d5!	f6

24...♗c7 25 ♘b5! ♖xd5 26 ♘xc7 ♖ad8 27 ♘xd5 ♖xd5 leads to an equal game.

25	Rd2	h5
26	Qg2	Rd7
27	c4	Rad8
28	c5	Ba5
29	b4	Bc7
30	h3	Be6
31	Red1	

31	...	e4!
32	Qxe4	Qxe4
33	Nxe4	Rxd2
34	Rxd2	Rxd2
35	Nxd2	Bxh3?!

Black captures the wrong pawn. After 35...Bxa2! 36 Bb2 Bd5 his position is better.

36	Ne4	Be6
37	Nd6	Bxd6

37...Bd5 looks stronger. Now White forces a draw.

38	cxd6	Kf7
39	b5	Ke8
40	d7+!	Kxd7
41	Bf8	g6
42	b6!	a5
43	a3	Kc6
44	Be7	Kxb6

45	Bxf6	Kb5
46	f4	Ka4
47	Be7	
	draw agreed	

Game 29
Tiviakov–Andersson
Haninge 1992

1	e4	e6
2	d4	d5
3	Nd2	c5
4	exd5	Qxd5
5	Ngf3	cxd4
6	Bc4	Qd6
7	0-0	Nf6
8	Nb3	Nc6
9	Nbxd4	Nxd4
10	Nxd4	Bd7
11	b3	Be7
12	a4	a6
13	Re1	Qc7
14	Qf3	0-0

14...0-0-0 can also be met by 15 Nf5, with the amusing variation 15...Bb4 16 Bf4 Qc6 17 Qc3!!

15	Nf5	Bd8

After 15...Rfe8 16 Nxe7+ Rxe7 there is the unpleasant pin 17 Bg5, while 15...Bb4 is very strongly met by 16 Nh6+! Kh8 17 Bb2.

16	Nxg7!?	

A double-edged sacrifice, although White is not in fact taking too much of a risk, since it is practically impossible for Black to escape from the pin without loss of material. Much more prosaic is 16 Bf4 Qc6 17 Qxc6 Bxc6 18 Nd4 with slightly the more active game.

16	...	♔xg7
17	♗b2	♖g8

The universal defence against the ♘f5xg7 attack. Black urgently evacuates his king, since continuations such as 17...♗c6 18 ♕g4+

♔h8 19 ♕h4 or 17...♗e7 18 ♕g4+ ♔h8 19 ♕h4 do not enable him to escape from the pin.

18 g3

As shown by Tiviakov, the only way to maintain the initiative was by 18 ♖e4! ♗c6 19 ♗xf6+ ♔f8! (not 19...♗xf6 20 ♖g4+ ♔f8 21 ♖xg8+ ♔xg8 22 ♕xf6) 20 ♖ae1 ♖g6 21 ♗xd8 ♖xd8 22 g3 ♗xe4 23 ♖xe4.

18	...	♗e7
19	♖ad1	♗c6
20	♕h5	♖ad8
21	♗e5	♖xd1
22	♖xd1	♕c8
23	♕h4	♖d8
24	♕g5+	♔f8
25	♖e1	♘e8
26	♕h5	

draw agreed

14   10...a6 – Introduction

1	e4	e6
2	d4	d5
3	♘d2	c5
4	exd5	♕xd5
5	♘gf3	cxd4
6	♗c4	♕d6
7	0-0	♘f6
8	♘b3	♘c6
9	♘bxd4	♘xd4
10	♘xd4	a6

This move is more popular than 10...♗d7, since it is more versatile. Black takes immediate control of b5, prepares a post for his queen, and in some cases can aim for the extended fianchetto after ...b7-b5, while retaining all the possible ideas examined earlier.

White has tried a whole range of replies: **11 a4** (Chapter 15), **11 c3** (Chapter 16), **11 b3** (Chapter 17), **11 ♗b3** (Chapter 18) and **11 ♖e1** (Chapter 19).

Here we will consider one less usual possibility:

11 ♗e3

White defends his knight, but this move does not have any serious thematic significance, and it allows Black to mobilise his forces successfully.

11	...	♕c7
12	♗b3	

12 ♕e2 ♗d7 13 ♖ad1 ♗d6 14 h3 0-0 15 ♗g5 ♔h8 16 ♗b3 ♗f4= (Akopian-Djurhuus, Santiago 1990).

12	...	♗d6
13	h3	0-0
14	♕e2	

14 c3?! e5 15 ♘f3 e4 16 ♘d4 ♕e7∓ (Almasi-Luther, Kecskemet 1993).

14	...	♗d7
15	♖ad1	♖ac8=

Meister-Doroshkevich (USSR 1988).

15   10...a6 11 a4

1	e4	e6
2	d4	d5
3	♘d2	c5
4	exd5	♛xd5
5	♘gf3	cxd4
6	♗c4	♛d6
7	0-0	♘f6
8	♘b3	♘c6
9	♘bxd4	♘xd4
10	♘xd4	a6
11	a4	

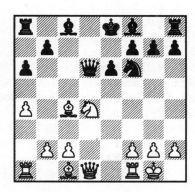

White radically prevents a possible ...b7-b5, and in some cases threatens to fix Black's queenside by a4-a5. Naturally, in this situation Black can hardly venture queenside castling.

His main continuations are **11... ♛c7 (15.1)** and **11...♗d7 (15.2)**, after which he usually plans to develop his bishop at d6.

15.1

(1 e4 e6 2 d4 d5 3 ♘d2 c5 4 exd5 ♛xd5 5 ♘gf3 cxd4 6 ♗c4 ♛d6 7 0-0 ♘f6 8 ♘b3 ♘c6 9 ♘bxd4 ♘xd4 10 ♘xd4 a6 11 a4)

11 ... ♛c7

12 ♛e2

12 b3 ♗d6 13 h3 0–0 14 ♗b2 e5 15 ♘f3 ♗f5 16 ♛e2 ♖fe8= (Upmark-Wikstrom, Sweden 1995).

12 ... ♗d6

13 h3

13 ♘f5 ♗xh2+ 14 ♔h1:

(a) 14...0-0? 15 ♘xg7 ♗f4 (15... ♔xg7 16 f4! ♗g3 17 ♖a3±) 16 ♘h5 ♘xh5 17 ♛xh5 ♛xc4∓ (Stromberg-Wikstrom, Sweden 1995);

(b) 14...♔f8 15 ♘g3! (15 ♘xg7?! h5! 16 g3 ♘g4 17 ♘xh5

♕c6+∓) 15...h5∞ (Van der Wiel-
Glek, Tilburg 1994) – *Game 30*.

    13 ...   0-0

    14 ♖d1

    (a) 14 ♗g5 ♗h2+ (14...b6 15
♖fd1 – 14 ♖d1) 15 ♔h1 ♗f4 16
♗xf4 (16 ♗xf6 gxf6∓) 16...♕xf4 17
♖fd1±;

    (b) 14 a5!?

    14 ...   b6

    15 ♗g5   ♗h2+

15...♖e8? 16 ♗xf6 gxf6 17
♘f5!± (A.Sokolov-Yudasin, Nikolaev 1983) – *Game 31*.

    16 ♔h1

16 ♔f1:

    (a) 16...♗f4 17 ♗xf4 ♕xf4 18
♕f3 ♕xf3 19 ♘xf3 ♗d7 Δ
...b6-b5=;

    (b) 16...♗e5=.

    16 ...   ♗e5

    17 ♖a3   ♗b7

    18 ♖e3   ♗f4=

Ljubojevic-Hübner (Wijk aan
Zee 1988) – *Game 32*.

15.2

(1 e4 e6 2 d4 d5 3 ♘d2 c5 4 exd5
♕xd5 5 ♘gf3 cxd4 6 ♗c4 ♕d6 7
0-0 ♘f6 8 ♘b3 ♘c6 9 ♘bxd4
♘xd4 10 ♘xd4 a6 11 a4)

    11 ...   ♗d7

    12 b3

12 ♖e1 ♕c7 13 ♕e2 ♗c5 14 c3
♗xd4 15 cxd4 ♖c8 16 b3 0-0 17
♗a3 ♖fe8 18 ♖ac1 ♗c6 19 ♕e5
♖ed8= (Anand-Andersson, Cannes
1989).

    12 ...   ♕c7

    13 ♗b2

13 ♕e2 ♗d6 14 h3 0-0 15 ♗b2
e5 16 ♘f3 e4 17 ♘d2 ♗h2+ 18
♔h1 ♗e5 19 ♗xe5 ♕xe5 20 a5 (20
♖fe1 ♖ae8 21 ♕e3 ♕c7 22 ♗f1
♖e6∓, Hellers-Korchnoi, Stockholm
1987) 20...♖ae8 21 ♖fe1 ♔h8 22
♕e3 ♕h5∓ (Zapata-Lobron, Moscow 1989).

    13 ...   ♗d6

    14 h3   0-0

    15 ♕f3   ♗e5

    16 ♖fe1   ♗c6

    17 ♕e2   ♗e4=

Van Wely-Vaisser (Brussels Zonal
1993).

Game 30
Van der Wiel–Glek
Tilburg 1994

    1 e4   e6

    2 d4   d5

    3 ♘d2   c5

4	exd5	♕xd5
5	♘gf3	cxd4
6	♗c4	♕d6
7	0-0	♘f6
8	♘b3	♘c6
9	♘bxd4	♘xd4
10	♘xd4	a6
11	a4	♕c7
12	♕e2	♗d6
13	♘f5	

Played under the influence of modern concepts, where in a number of cases the capture of the h2 pawn is considered a serious loss of time. The main continuation is 13 h3.

13	...	♗xh2+
14	♔h1	♔f8!

Of course, if 14...0-0 there would have followed 15 ♘xg7!, when Black has nothing better than to retreat his bishop with 15...♗f4 (15...♔xg7? 16 f4! ♗g3 17 ♖a3), after which 16 ♘h5 leaves White with an attack. But 14...♗f4 15 ♘xg7+ ♔f8 16 ♕f3 e5 was also interesting.

Now, however, 15 ♘xg7? favours Black after 15...h5! 16 g3 ♘g4.

15	♘g3	h5
16	♔xh2	h4
17	♔g1	hxg3
18	fxg3	e5!

Fresh resources are more important than winning a pawn. After 18...♕xg3 19 ♗f4 ♕h4 20 ♖a3! ♕h1+ 21 ♔f2 the king finds shelter and the initiative passes to White.

19	b3

In view of the threats along the a7-g1 diagonal, it would have been more advisable to keep the bishop close to the king – 19 ♗e3!

19	...	♗e6!
20	♗a3+?	

Of course, on 20 ♗xe6 there follows 20...♕b6+ 21 ♗e3 ♕xe6, but White clearly does not sense the danger, otherwise he would have decided to go into the ending after 20 a5 ♗xc4 21 ♕xc4 ♕xc4 22 bxc4, with play against the b7 pawn.

20	...	♔g8
21	♗xe6	♕b6+
22	♕f2	♕xe6
23	♕f5	♕b6+
24	♕f2	♕e6

Black understandably avoids the threefold repetition of the position, but here he could have gone into a favourable ending: 24...♕xf2+ 25 ♖xf2 ♘g4 26 ♖d2 ♖e8 27 ♖d7 e4 28 ♖e1 e3 (Van der Wiel).

25	♕f5	♖e8
26	♖ad1	♖h5
27	♕xe6	♖xe6
28	♖d8+	♔h7
29	♖b8	b6
30	♗c1	♔g6

The rapid advance of the e-pawn could have caused White more problems: 30...e4! 31 ♖b7 e3 32 ♖xf7 e2 33 ♖e1 ♖d5 and wins. His only option would have been to block the pawn with 31 ♗e3 ♘d5 32 ♖e1.

31	♖b7	e4
32	g4!	♖d5!

Not yielding to the temptation of 32...♘xg4 33 ♖fxf7 e3? 34 ♖xg7+.

33	g5	♘d7

But here 33...♘g4 34 ♖fxf7 e3! 35 ♖xg7+ ♔f5 was now possible.

34	♗e3	♖c6
35	c4	♖d3
36	♖e1	a5

36...♘e5!, aiming for g4, was more vigorous.

37	♗f2	♖e6
38	♗e3	f6?

Even here it was not yet too late for 38...♘e5 or 38...♘c5.

39	gxf6	gxf6
40	♔f1!	f5?!

One gains the impression that Black simply cannot bring himself to play his knight to e5, although by now this was the last chance: 40...♘e5! 41 ♖xb6 ♖xb6 42 ♗xb6 ♖xb3 43 ♗xa5 ♘xc4, retaining some advantage.

41	♔e2	♘e5
42	♖h1	♘g4
43	♗f4	♖xb3
44	♖h8	♖b2+
45	♔e1	e3
46	♖g8+	♔f6
47	♖f8+	♔g6
48	♖g8+	

draw agreed

Game 31
A.Sokolov–Yudasin
USSR Championship Semi-Final
Nikolaev 1983

1	e4	e6
2	d4	d5
3	♘d2	c5
4	♘gf3	cxd4
5	exd5	♕xd5
6	♗c4	♕d6
7	0-0	♘f6
8	♘b3	♘c6
9	♘bxd4	♘xd4
10	♘xd4	a6
11	a4	♕c7
12	♕e2	♗d6
13	h3	0-0
14	♗g5	b6
15	♖fd1	♖e8?

This was one of the first attempts at playing this variation. At that time White's attack was not feared, otherwise Black would have found the defensive manoeuvre 15...♗h2+ 16 ♔h1 ♗e5.

16	♗xf6	gxf6
17	♘f5!	♗f8
18	♖a3	♔h8
19	♖g3	♕f4
20	♗d3!	

As though in accordance with a pre-arranged timetable, White's pieces join the attack on the kingside.

Sokolov is not tempted by the win of the exchange: 20 ♘d6 ♗xd6 21 ♖xd6 ♕xd6 22 ♕g4 ♕f8 23 ♕f3 ♕e7 24 ♕xa8 ♗b7∞.

20 ... ♖a7

After 20...♗b7? 21 ♕h5 Black has no defence.

21 ♖e1 ♖d8
22 ♖g4 ♕e5

Against 22...♕c7 Sokolov had prepared 23 ♖c4 ♕e5 24 ♕d1 ♕xb2 25 ♕h5 exf5 26 ♖xc8! ♖xc8 27 ♕xf5, winning.

23	♖g8+!	♔xg8
24	♕g4+	♔h8
25	♖xe5	fxe5
26	♕h4	♖d5
27	♘e3	♖xd3
28	cxd3	♖d7
29	♘g4	

Black resigns

Game 32
Ljubojevic–Hübner
Wijk aan Zee 1988

1	e4	e6
2	d4	d5
3	♘d2	c5
4	♘gf3	cxd4
5	exd5	♕xd5
6	♗c4	♕d6
7	0-0	♘f6
8	♘b3	♘c6
9	♘bxd4	♘xd4
10	♘xd4	a6
11	a4	♕c7
12	♕e2	♗d6
13	h3	0-0
14	♖d1	b6
15	♗g5	♗h2+
16	♔h1	♗e5

Of course, not 16...♗b7? 17 ♗xf6 gxf6 18 ♘xe6. The present game demonstrates Black's defensive possibilities.

17	♖a3	♗b7
18	♖e3	♗f4

19 ♗xf4

The tempting 19 ♘xe6 fxe6 20 ♖xe6 ♔h8 21 ♗xf6 ♖xf6 22 ♖e7 ♕c6 23 ♗d5 ♕xd5 24 ♖xd5 ♗xd5 leaves Black with too much for the queen (Hübner).

19	...	♕xf4
20	c3	♖fd8
21	♔g1	a5
22	♖e1	

22 ♖ed3 is well met by 22...♕e4.

22	...	♗d5
23	♖e5	♖ac8
24	♗a6	♖c5
25	♗b5	g6
26	♕d3?!	

Careless. White fails to sense the danger stemming from Black's centralised pieces. He should have driven away the queen by 26 g3 ♕h6 27 h4 ♕f8, with chances for both sides.

26	...	♖dc8
27	♖1e3	♗b7
28	♘e2	♕h4
29	♖xc5	bxc5!

Black aims to cut off the bishop at b5 by ...c5-c4, which is possible after 30 ♕d6?! ♘e4 31 ♕f4 ♕xf4 32 ♘xf4 c4.

30	♖e5	♘d5
31	♕d2	♖d8
32	♕g5	♕xg5
33	♖xg5	f5?

This weakens the position too much. 33...f6 was more accurate, retaining the better chances.

34	♖g3	♘b6
35	♖e3	♔f7
	draw agreed	

16   10...a6 11 c3

1	e4	e6
2	d4	d5
3	♘d2	c5
4	exd5	♕xd5
5	♘gf3	cxd4
6	♗c4	♕d6
7	0-0	♘f6
8	♘b3	♘c6
9	♘bxd4	♘xd4
10	♘xd4	a6
11	c3	

White frees his queen from the need to defend his knight at d4, but Black gains a tempo to play his queen to its main post.

    11 ... ♕c7

Here White's main continuations are the prophylactic retreat **12 ♗b3 (16.1)** and the developing **12 ♕e2 (16.2)**.

After the retreat 12 ♗d3 Black has an easy game: 12...♗d6 13 h3 ♗d7 14 ♖e1 (14 ♕f3 ♗h2+ 15 ♔h1 ♗e5 16 ♘g5 h6 17 ♗h4 ♗xd4 18 cxd4 ♗c6∓, Relange-Vaisser, France 1991) 14...0-0 15 ♗g5 ♘d5 16 ♕h5 g6 17 ♕h4 ♗f4=.

16.1

(1 e4 e6 2 d4 d5 3 ♘d2 c5 4 exd5 ♕xd5 5 ♘gf3 cxd4 6 ♗c4 ♕d6 7 0-0 ♘f6 8 ♘b3 ♘c6 9 ♘bxd4 ♘xd4 10 ♘xd4 a6 11 c3 ♕c7)

12	♗b3	♗d6
13	h3	0-0

    14 ♖e1

(a) 14 ♕f3 b6 15 ♖e1 ♗b7 16 ♕d3 ♖fe8 (16...♗h2+ 17 ♔h1 ♗e5=) 17 ♗g5 ♘d5 18 ♘f5 ♗h2+ 19 ♔h1 (Arkell-Levitt, London 1988) 19...♗f4=;

(b) 14 ♗g5:

(b1) 14...♗f4 15 ♗xf6 gxf6 16 ♕g4+ ♔h8 17 ♕h4 ♗g5 18 ♕h5 ♖g8= (Nunn-Speelman, London 1984);

(b2) 14...♘e4 15 ♗e3 ♗h2+ 16 ♔h1 ♗f4= (Jansa-Glek, Cattolica 1993).

14 ...   b5

14...e5 15 ♘c2 h6 16 ♘e3 ♖d8 (16...♖e8!? 17 ♘d5 ♘xd5 18 ♗xd5 ♖b8 19 ♗e3 ♔h8 Δ ...f7-f5∞) 17 ♘c4 ♗e6 18 ♕e2 ♖ac8 19 ♘xd6 ♕xd6 20 ♖d1 ♕c6! ½-½ (Zapata-Nogueiras, Wijk aan Zee 1987).

15 ♗g5   ♗b7!

15...♘d7 16 ♖xe6!

16 ♗c2

16 ♗xf6 gxf6 17 ♕g4+ ♔h8 18 ♕h4 ♖g8!∓→.

16 ...   ♘d5

17 ♕h5

17 ♕g4 ♖fe8 18 ♕h4 g6 19 ♗e4 f5= (Akopian-Levitt, Groningen 1990).

17 ...   g6
18 ♕h4   ♗h2+

19 ♔h1   ♗f4
20 ♗e4   ♖ab8

20...♗xg5!? 21 ♕xg5 ♖ad8 Δ ...♖d7, ...♕f4=.

21 ♖ad1   ♗xg5
22 ♕xg5   ♕f4

22...♘b6? 23 ♗xb7 ♕xb7 24 ♘f3± (Adams-Gulko, Groningen PCA 1993) – **Game 33**.

23 ♕xf4   ♘xf4=

16.2

(1 e4 e6 2 d4 d5 3 ♘d2 c5 4 exd5 ♕xd5 5 ♘gf3 cxd4 6 ♗c4 ♕d6 7 0-0 ♘f6 8 ♘b3 ♘c6 9 ♘bxd4 ♘xd4 10 ♘xd4 a6 11 c3 ♕c7)

12 ♕e2

12 ...   ♗d6

(a) 12...♗e7 13 ♗g5 0-0 14 ♗b3 h6 15 ♗h4 ♗d7 16 ♖fe1 ♖ae8= (Zapata-Smyslov, Subotica Interzonal 1987);

(b) 12...♗d7 13 a4 ♗d6 (13...♗c5 14 ♗g5 0-0 15 ♗d3

♗xd4 16 cxd4 ♘d5 17 ♖a3 ♘f4 18 ♕g4 e5 19 ♕g3±, Zapata-Moran, Cali 1990) 14 h3 0-0 15 ♗g5 ♕c5 16 ♗xf6 gxf6 17 ♖fd1 ♖fd8 18 ♗d3 f5 19 ♕h5± (Tolnai-Polyakin, New York 1993).

13 h3

(a) 13 g3 0-0 14 ♗g5 ♘e4= (Zarnicki-Danielian, Buenos Aires 1992);

(b) 13 ♘f5?! ♗xh2+ 14 ♔h1 0–0 15 ♘h6+ (Dobosz-Ornstein, Gausdal 1979) 15...gxh6 16 g3 b5 17 ♗d3 ♗xg3∓ (Ornstein);

(c) 13 ♗g5 ♗xh2+ 14 ♔h1 ♗f4 15 ♗xf6 gxf6 16 ♗xe6 fxe6 17 ♘xe6 ♗xe6 18 ♕xe6+ ♔f8 19 ♕xf6+ ♔g8= (Liang Jinrong-Brunner, Lucerne 1989).

13 ... 0-0

(a) 13...b5 14 ♗d3 0-0 15 a4 b4 16 cxb4 ♗xb4 17 ♖d1 ♗b7= (Smagin-Levitt, Hastings 1990);

(b) 13...♗h2+ 14 ♔h1 ♗f4 15 ♗xf4 ♕xf4 16 ♗b3 0-0= (Hracek-Rugele, Manila Olympiad 1992).

14 ♗b3

(a) 14 ♗d3 ♗d7 15 ♗g5 ♘d5 16 ♕e4?! (16 ♖fe1=) 16...f5! 17 ♕f3 h6 18 ♗d2 ♘f6∓ (Blatny-Lautier, Adelaide 1988);

(b) 14 ♖d1 b5? (14...♗h2+ 15 ♔h1 ♗f4=) 15 ♗d3 ♗b7 16 a4!± (A.Sokolov-Speelman, Reykjavik 1988) – *Game 34*;

(c) 14 ♗g5:

(c1) 14...b5?! 15 ♗d3 ♗b7 16 ♗xf6 gxf6 17 ♕g4+ ♔h8 18 ♕h5± (Rogic-Psakhis, Zagreb 1993);

(c2) 14...♔h8 15 ♖ad1 ♗h2+ 16 ♔h1 ♗f4 17 ♗xf4 ♕xf4 18 ♘f3 b5= (Spasov-Akopian, Debrecen 1992);

(c3) 14...♘e4! 15 ♗h4 (15 ♕xe4 ♕xc4=) 15...♘d2! 16 ♕xd2 ♕xc4∓ (Kosashvili-Holzke, Biel 1989).

14 ... b5

(a) 14...e5 15 ♘f3 e4 16 ♘d4 ♕c5= (Rozentalis-Akopian, USSR 1988);

(b) 14...h6!? 15 ♕f3 b6! 16 ♗xh6? (16 ♕xa8∞; 16 ♕c6=) 16...♗b7 17 ♕e3 gxh6 18 ♕xh6 ♗h2+ 19 ♔h1 ♕f4∓ (Mohr-Belyavsky, Maribor 1996).

15	♗g5	♗b7
16	♖ad1	♘e4
17	♗c1	♖ae8
18	a4	b4=

Xie Jun-Psakhis (Moscow 1992).

Game 33
Adams–Gulko
Groningen (PCA) 1993

1	e4	e6
2	d4	d5
3	♘d2	c5

4	exd5	♕xd5
5	♘gf3	cxd4
6	♗c4	♕d6
7	0-0	♘f6
8	♘b3	♘c6
9	♘bxd4	♘xd4
10	♘xd4	a6
11	c3	♕c7
12	♗b3	♗d6
13	h3	0-0
14	♖e1	b5

14...e5 15 ♘c2 h6 16 ♘e3 and then 16...♖d8 or 16...♖e8 would seem to be safer.

| 15 | ♗g5 | ♗b7 |
| 16 | ♗c2 | |

After 16 ♗xf6 gxf6 17 ♕g4+ ♔h8 18 ♕h4 ♖g8! White himself would come under attack. But now this exchange is threatened.

16	...	♘d5
17	♕h5	g6
18	♕h4	♗h2+
19	♔h1	♗f4

A standard manoeuvre for neutralising White's active bishop.

20	♗e4	♖ab8
21	♖ad1	♗xg5
22	♕xg5	♘b6?

Black does not sense the danger, otherwise he would have neutralised the queen by 22...♕f4.

| 23 | ♗xb7 | ♕xb7 |
| 24 | ♘f3 | |

Now, in view of the threat of an attack on h7, Black is forced into a gruelling defence.

| 24 | ... | ♘d5 |

After 24...♔g7 White begins play on the dark squares: 25 ♕e5+

♔g8 26 ♘g5, with the threat of ♘e4.

25	♕h6	♖fd8
26	♖d4	♕e7
27	♖h4	♘f6

| 28 | ♘e5! | |

The culmination of the attack. White threatens not only ♘g4, but also ♘c6.

28	...	♖d6
29	♘g4	♖bd8
30	♘xf6+	♕xf6
31	♕xh7+	♔f8
32	♕h6+	♔g8
33	♖f4	♕g7
34	♕g5	♖d2
35	♕e7	♕f8?

Overlooking White's threat, but equally after 35...♖2d7 36 ♕c5 the weakness of Black's queenside would have made his position critical.

36	♖xe6!	fxe6
37	♕xe6+	♔g7
38	♕e5+	♔g8
39	♖xf8+	♖xf8

| 40 | ♕g5 | ♖fxf2 |

The ending is hopeless for Black, since his rooks are unable to cope with the passed pawns that White creates on opposite wings.

41	♕xg6+	♔h8
42	♕h6+	♔g8
43	♕xa6	♖xb2
44	a3	♔h7
45	♕c6	♖fc2
46	h4	♖c1+
47	♔h2	♖bc2
48	♕xb5	♖xc3
49	a4	♖c4
50	♕h5+	♔g7
51	♕g5+	♔h7
52	a5	♖c7
53	a6	♖1c6
54	♕e3	♖c4
55	♕d3+	♔g7
56	♕g3+	

Black resigns

Game 34
A.Sokolov–Speelman
Reykjavik 1988

1	e4	e6
2	d4	d5
3	♘d2	c5
4	exd5	♕xd5
5	♘gf3	cxd4
6	♗c4	♕d6
7	0-0	♘f6
8	♘b3	♘c6
9	♘bxd4	♘xd4
10	♘xd4	a6
11	c3	♕c7
12	♕e2	♗d6
13	h3	0-0
14	♖d1	b5?!

Somewhat premature, since it allows White to exploit the weakening of the queenside. 14...♗h2+ 15 ♔h1 ♗f4 is safer.

| 15 | ♗d3 | ♗b7 |
| 16 | a4! | b4 |

After 16...bxa4 Black has problems with his weak a6 pawn: 17 ♖xa4 a5 18 ♗g5 ♗e7 19 ♖da1.

17	cxb4	♗xb4
18	♗g5	♘d5
19	♖ac1	♕d7
20	♕e4	g6
21	♗h6	♖fc8
22	♕e5	♗f8
23	♗xf8	♖xf8
24	♘b3!	♕xa4
25	♘c5	♕b4

| 26 | ♗e4?! |

Procrastination. White could have won more quickly by 26 ♖c4! ♕b6 (26...♕b5 27 ♘xe6 fxe6 28 ♖c7! winning the queen) 27 ♘d7.

| 26 | ... | ♖fe8 |

27	♘d7	♖ad8
28	♖xd5!	exd5
29	♘f6+	♔f8
30	♘xh7+	♔g8
31	♘f6+	♔f8
32	♘h7+	

In time trouble White rejects 32 ♘xe8 which would have retained the advantage (in view of 32...♖xe8 33 ♕h8+ ♔e7 34 ♕h4+ ♔f8 35 ♕h6+), and allows a threefold repetition of the position.

32	...	♔g8
33	♘f6+	♔f8
34	♘h7+	

draw agreed

17   10...a6 11 b3

1	e4	e6
2	d4	d5
3	♘d2	c5
4	exd5	♕xd5
5	♘gf3	cxd4
6	♗c4	♕d6
7	0-0	♘f6
8	♘b3	♘c6
9	♘bxd4	♘xd4
10	♘xd4	a6
11	b3	

A fairly thematic continuation – White defends his bishop at c4 (after ...♕c7) and also aims his dark-square bishop at the kingside. But Black gains the opportunity for the extended fianchetto after ...b7-b5, which helps him in turn to create threats on the kingside.

    11   ...   ♕c7

In this line too the queen usually makes way for the bishop. But the more modest 11...♗e7 also looks perfectly sound, passing the attacking functions to the other bishop after 12 ♗b2 b5 (12...0-0 – 10...♗e7 11 b3 0-0 12 ♗b2 a6, Chapter 10), for example:

(a) 13 ♕f3!? ♖b8 14 ♗d3 ♗b7 15 ♕h3∞ (Ghidzavu-Padevski, Varna 1973);

(b) 13 ♗d3 ♗b7 14 ♖e1 0-0 15 ♕e2 ♖fe8 16 ♖ad1 ♕c7 17 ♘f3 ♗b4 18 ♖f1 ♗c3= (Quillan-Levitt, British Ch 1993).

For 11...♗d7, see section 13.1.

12 ♕e2 (17.1)
12 ♗b2 (17.2)

    12 ♕f3?! ♗d6:

(a) 13 h3 0-0 14 ♗b2 b5! 15 ♗xb5 (15 ♕xa8 ♗b7∓) 15...e5! 16 ♗c6 ♖b8 17 ♘e2 ♖b6 18 ♗e4 ♘xe4 19 ♕xe4 ♗b7∓ (Brandner-Santos, Tunja 1989);

(b) 13 ♖e1 0–0 14 ♗b2 b5! 15 ♗d3 ♗b7 16 ♕h3 ♖fe8 17 ♘f5!? (17 ♘xb5?! axb5 18 ♗xf6 gxf6 19 ♕xh7+ ♔f8∓) 17...exf5 18 ♗xf6 ♗e4!= (Bohak).

17.1

(1 e4 e6 2 d4 d5 3 ♘d2 c5 4 exd5 ♕xd5 5 ♘gf3 cxd4 6 ♗c4 ♕d6 7 0-0 ♘f6 8 ♘b3 ♘c6 9 ♘bxd4 ♘xd4 10 ♘xd4 a6 11 b3 ♕c7)

12   ♕e2

12...♗d6 (17.11)
12...♗c5 (17.12)

(a) 12...b5 13 ♗d3 ♗c5 14
♘f5?! (14 ♗b2∞) 14...0-0 15 ♘xg7
♔xg7 16 ♗b2 ♖g8!∓ (Kaiszauri-
Ornstein, Eksjo 1981) – *Game 35*;
(b) 12...♗d7?! – 10...♗d7 11 b3
a6 12 ♗b2 ♕c7 (section 13.1).

17.11

(1 e4 e6 2 d4 d5 3 ♘d2 c5 4 exd5
♕xd5 5 ♘gf3 cxd4 6 ♗c4 ♕d6 7
0-0 ♘f6 8 ♘b3 ♘c6 9 ♘bxd4
♘xd4 10 ♘xd4 a6 11 b3 ♕c7 12
♕e2)

12   ...   ♗d6
13   ♘f5   ♗xh2+
14   ♔h1   0-0
14...♕e5?! 15 ♘xg7+ ♔f8 16
♗h6 ♕xe2 17 ♗xe2 ♗e5 18 ♘h5+
♔e8 19 ♗g7! ♗xa1 20 ♗xh8 ♘xh5
21 ♗xa1 ♘f4 22 ♗f3± (Golubovic-
Bohak, Bled 1994).

15   ♘xg7   ♕e5
(a) 15...♔xg7? 16 ♗b2 ♕f4 17
♕h5±±;
(b) 15...♗e5 16 ♗h6 ♗xa1 17
♖xa1 ♕c5 18 ♖d1 (18 ♖e1⩲, Euwe)
18...b5 19 ♗e3 ♕e5 20 f4 ♘e4!∞
(Tseshkovsky-Shtyrenkov, Belore-
chensk 1989).
16   g3
16 ♗h6 ♕xe2 17 ♗xe2 ♗e5=.
16   ...   ♕xa1
16...♕xe2? 17 ♗xe2± (Geller-
Stahlberg, Gothenburg Interzonal
1955).
17   c3   b5
18   ♗d3   ♖d8=
Rubin-Glek (corr. 1989) – *Game
36*.

17.12

(1 e4 e6 2 d4 d5 3 ♘d2 c5 4 exd5
♕xd5 5 ♘gf3 cxd4 6 ♗c4 ♕d6 7
0-0 ♘f6 8 ♘b3 ♘c6 9 ♘bxd4
♘xd4 10 ♘xd4 a6 11 b3 ♕c7 12
♕e2)

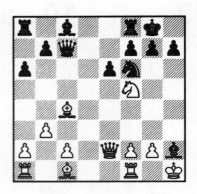

12 ... **♗c5**

12 ♗b2

13 ♗b2
13 ♘f5?! 0-0 14 ♘xg7 ♔xg7
(14...♗d4 15 ♗h6 ♗xa1 16 ♖xa1∞)
15 ♗b2 (Geller-Kindermann, Dortmund 1989) 15...♖g8!∓.
    13 ... **0-0**
    14 ♖ad1
14 ♘f3 b5 15 ♗d3 ♗b7 16 ♘e5!
(16 ♘g5?! ♕c6!=) 16...♖ad8 17
♖ad1 ♗a8 △ 18...♕b7.
    14 ... **b5**
    15 ♗d3 **♗b7**
    16 ♘f3
16 ♘xb5? (△ 16...axb5 17 ♗xf6)
16...♕c6+∓.
    16 ... **♕f4=**
Kotronias-Kindermann (Debrecen 1989) – *Game 37*.

17.2

(1 e4 e6 2 d4 d5 3 ♘d2 c5 4 exd5
♕xd5 5 ♘gf3 cxd4 6 ♗c4 ♕d6 7
0-0 ♘f6 8 ♘b3 ♘c6 9 ♘bxd4
♘xd4 10 ♘xd4 a6 11 b3 ♕c7)

12 ... **♗d6**
12...♗d7 – 10...♗d7 11 b3 ♕c7
12 ♗b2 a6 (section 13.1).

13 h3 (17.21)
13 ♘f3 (17.22)

17.21

(1 e4 e6 2 d4 d5 3 ♘d2 c5 4 exd5
♕xd5 5 ♘gf3 cxd4 6 ♗c4 ♕d6 7
0-0 ♘f6 8 ♘b3 ♘c6 9 ♘bxd4
♘xd4 10 ♘xd4 a6 11 b3 ♕c7 12
♗b2 ♗d6)

    13 h3 **0-0**
    14 ♗d3
    (a) 14 ♖e1 b5 15 ♗f1?! (15
♗d3!?∞) 15...♖d8 16 ♕e2 ♗b7∓
(Lobron-Petrosian, Plovdiv 1983) –
Game 38;
    (b) 14 a4?! e5 15 ♘f3 e4! (15...
♗d7 16 ♕e2 e4 17 ♘d2 ♗e5=,
Blehn-S.Ivanov, Cappelle la Grande

1996) 16 ♘d4 ♗d7∓ (Tiviakov-
Dreev, Podolsk 1992) – *Game 39*;
  (c) 14 ♕f3!? Δ 14...e5 15 ♘f5∞.

14   ...   b5
15   ♘f3

15 c4 bxc4 16 ♗xc4 ♗h2+ 17
♔h1 ♗f4= (Dvoiris-Glek, Kharkov
1986).

15   ...   ♗b7
16   ♕e2   ♖fe8
17   ♗xf6
17 ♘e5 ♘d5∓.
17   ...   gxf6
18   ♗e4   ♗xe4
19   ♕xe4   f5
20   ♕h4   ♕e7=

Mannion-Lalic (Hastings 1995).

17.22

(1 e4 e6 2 d4 d5 3 ♘d2 c5 4 exd5
♕xd5 5 ♘gf3 cxd4 6 ♗c4 ♕d6 7
0-0 ♘f6 8 ♘b3 ♘c6 9 ♘bxd4
♘xd4 10 ♘xd4 a6 11 b3 ♕c7 12
♗b2 ♗d6)

13   ♘f3

13   ...   b5
13...b6 14 ♖e1 (14 ♕e2!? ♗b7
15 a4±) 14...♗b7 15 ♗d3 ♘d5 16
a4 0-0-0 17 g3 ♔b8= (Timosh-
chenko-Danielian,   Cappelle   la
Grande 1994) – *Game 40*.

14   ♗d3   ♗b7
15   ♖e1

15 a4 b4 16 ♗xf6 gxf6 17 ♖e1
♖d8= (Akopian-Glek, Novogorsk
1990).

15   ...   0-0
16   ♘e5!?

  (a) 16 a4 ♖fd8 17 ♕e2 ♗b4 18
♖f1 bxa4 19 ♖xa4 a5= (Psakhis-
Chernin, USSR Ch 1987);
  (b) 16 ♗xf6 gxf6 17 ♗e4 ♖ad8
18 ♕e2 ♗c8!= Δ 19 h3?! (19 c4=)
19...f5 20 ♗d3 ♗b7 21 a4 ♗b4 22
♖ed1 ♗c3∓ (Ornstein).

16   ...   ♖ad8
16...♘d5!? 17 ♕h5 f5!=.
17   ♕e2   ♘d5!=
Tiviakov-Psakhis (Rostov 1993).

Game 35
Kaiszauri–Ornstein
Eksjo 1981

1	e4	e6
2	d4	d5
3	♘d2	c5
4	exd5	♕xd5
5	♘gf3	cxd4
6	♗c4	♕d6
7	0-0	♘f6
8	♘b3	♘c6
9	♘bxd4	♘xd4
10	♘xd4	a6
11	b3	♕c7
12	♕e2	b5

A rare, although not yet discredited continuation. Black usually plays 12...♗d6 or the more active 12...♗c5, after which 13 ♘f5?! 0-0 14 ♘xg7 is parried by the same method that was first demonstrated in the present game: 14...♔xg7 15 ♗b2 ♖g8!, while if 13 ♗b2, then 13...0-0 followed by ...b7-b5 is now possible.

13	♗d3	♗c5
14	♘f5?!	

14 ♗b2 was more prudent.

14	...	0-0
15	♘xg7	♔xg7
16	♗b2	♖g8!

16...♕f4? loses to 17 g3 ♕h6 18 ♕g4+ ♔h8 19 ♕e4.

17	♗e4	

The double pin created after 17 ♕f3 ♗e7 18 ♕g3+ ♕xg3 19 fxg3 cannot be exploited in view of 19...h5! But now too Black finds

defensive resources against the seemingly powerful attack.

17	...	♖a7
18	♕h5	h6
19	♖ad1	♗e7
20	♗e5	♗b7!
21	♖d4	

Also insufficient is 21 ♗xb7 ♕xb7 22 f3 ♕c8 23 ♖d4 ♔h7 24 ♕xf7+ ♖g7, or 21 f3 ♗xe4 22 fxe4 ♕xc2 23 ♖f2 ♕xe4 24 ♖df1 ♔h7 (Ornstein).

21	...	♗xe4
22	♖xe4	♕xc2!
23	♖g4+	♔f8
24	♕xh6+	♔e8
25	♖xg8+	♘xg8
26	♕h8	♕g6
27	♖c1	

The last dying embers of the attack. Against 27 ♗g7 Black has the defence 27...♗f8!

27	...	f6
28	♗b2	♔f7
29	♕h3	♖d7
30	♖e1	♕f5

31	g4	♕g6
32	♕f3	♕d3
33	♕c6	♖d6
34	♕c8	♕f3
35	g5	fxg5
36	♕c2	♕g4+
37	♔f1	♕f5
38	♕c3	♕d3+

White resigns

Game 36
Rubin–Glek
Correspondence 1989

1	e4	e6
2	d4	d5
3	♘d2	c5
4	exd5	♕xd5
5	♘gf3	cxd4
6	♗c4	♕d6
7	0-0	♘f6
8	♘b3	♘c6
9	♘bxd4	♘xd4
10	♘xd4	a6
11	b3	♕c7
12	♕e2	♗d6
13	♘f5	♗xh2+
14	♔h1	0-0
15	♘xg7	♕e5

In the given set-up 15...♔xg7? can be met by 16 ♗b2 ♕f4 17 ♕h5, but 15...♗e5 is also possible.

16	g3	♕xa1
17	c3	b5
18	♗d3	♖d8

Black could also have decided on 18...♕xc3 19 ♗b2 ♕c6+, when after 20 ♔xh2 e5! 21 ♘f5 ♗xf5 22 ♗xf5 ♖fe8 or 20 f3! e5! 21 ♕xe5 ♗b7! 22 ♕xf6 ♕xf6 23 ♗xf6

♖fd8! he consolidates his forces (Glek).

| 19 | ♗e4 | |

19 ♗d2 ♕xf1+! 20 ♕xf1 ♔xg7 is not dangerous for Black.

| 19 | ... | ♘xe4 |
| 20 | ♕xe4 | ♕xc3! |

Attack and defence are up to the mark. If 20...♖b8 White continues his attack with 21 ♕e5.

21	♘h5!	♕d3
22	♕g4+	♕g6
23	♕h4	♗b7+
24	♔xh2	e5
25	♗b2	♖e8!
26	♘f6+	♔g7
27	♘xe8+	♖xe8
28	♖c1	♕f5
29	♕f4	

White decides to play for a draw in an ending with opposite-colour bishops, since 29 f4? oversteps the bounds of risk in view of the possible ...♕e4 (after the prophylactic 29...h6).

| 29 | ... | ♔g6 |

30	♕xf5+	♔xf5
31	♖c7	♗d5
32	♖d7	♔e6
33	♖a7	♖c8
34	g4	♖c2
35	♖xa6+	♗c6
36	♔g3	f6
37	f4	♔d5
38	♗a1	e4
39	♖a7	e3
40	♖e7	♖g2+!
41	♔xg2	♔d6+
42	♔f1	♔xe7
43	♔e2	♗d7
44	f5	h5!
45	gxh5	♗xf5
46	♔xe3	♗g4
47	h6	♔f7
	draw agreed	

Game 37
Kotronias–Kindermann
Debrecen 1989

1	e4	e6
2	d4	d5
3	♘d2	c5
4	♘gf3	cxd4
5	exd5	♕xd5
6	♗c4	♕d6
7	0-0	♘f6
8	♘b3	♘c6
9	♘bxd4	♘xd4
10	♘xd4	a6
11	b3	♕c7
12	♕e2	♗c5
13	♗b2	0-0
14	♖ad1	b5
15	♗d3	♗b7

16	♘f3	♕f4
17	♘e5	

17 ♕e5 ♕xe5 18 ♘xe5 leads to an equal endgame.

17	...	♕g5
18	g3	♖ad8
19	a3?!	

An inexplicable move, which hands Black the initiative. With 19 ♗c1! White could have forced an equal ending after 19...♕h5 20 ♕xh5 ♘xh5.

19	...	♘d5!

Not only avoiding the exchange of queens, but also threatening ...♘f4, which is also possible after 20 ♗e4? ♘f4 21 ♕f3 ♘h3+, winning the f2 pawn.

20	♗c1	♕e7
21	♕e4	f5

21...g6 followed by ...f7-f6 is more prudent.

22	♕e1	

22	...	♗a8!

Preparing to set up a battery on the long diagonal (23 c4? ♘c3! 24

♕xc3 ♕b7). After 22...♗xa3 the
weakness of the e6 pawn is
exposed: 23 ♘c6! ♗xc6 24 ♗xa3
♕xa3 25 ♕xe6+ ♔h8 26 ♕xc6.

23	♗e2	♗xa3
24	♗xa3	♕xa3
25	c4	♘f6

25...bxc4 26 bxc4 ♘c3 was also
possible.

26	cxb5	axb5
27	♖xd8	♖xd8
28	♗xb5	♕xb3
29	♗c4	♕b7
30	f3	♕b6+
31	♕f2	♕xf2+
32	♖xf2	♗d5
33	♖d2	♖c8
34	♖d4?!	

With this pseudo-activity White
merely assists the advance of the
enemy king. It would have been
easier to hold the position after 34
♗e2.

34	...	♔f8
35	♔f2	♔e7
36	♗d3	♖a8!
37	g4	♔d6
38	♘f7+	♔c5
39	♖f4	

39 ♔e3 does not work in view of
39...e5! 40 ♘xe5 ♖e8 41 f4 ♘xg4+.

39	...	fxg4
40	fxg4	♖f8

White resigns

**Game 38
Lobron–Petrosian
*Plovdiv 1983***

1	e4	e6
2	d4	d5
3	♘d2	c5
4	exd5	♕xd5
5	♘gf3	cxd4
6	♗c4	♕d6
7	0-0	♘f6
8	♘b3	♘c6
9	♘bxd4	♘xd4
10	♘xd4	a6
11	b3	♕c7
12	♗b2	♗d6
13	h3	0-0
14	♖e1	b5
15	♗f1?!	

More natural and stronger is 15
♗d3, since now the initiative passes
to Black.

15	...	♖d8
16	♕e2	♗b7
17	c4	♗c5

Subtly perceiving the weakness
of the f2 pawn (in analogy with the
f7 pawn in a number of positions
from the Ruy Lopez), whereas by
trying to extract dividends from the
b8-h2 diagonal Black would have
risked losing the initiative: 17...
♘e4?! 18 ♕c2! ♗h2+ 19 ♔h1 ♕f4
20 ♖e2 ♗g3 21 fxg3 ♘xg3+ 22
♔g1 ♖xd4 23 ♖f2!± (Petrosian).

18	♖ad1	bxc4

18...♗b4 19 ♕e5!∞ would have
been a deviation from Black's goal.

19	♕xc4	♕b6
20	a3	a5

20...♗d5! was stronger, avoiding
the weakening of the b5 square.

21	♖e5	♖ac8
22	♕b5	

29	♖d3	♖b6
30	♗d4	♖b7
31	♘e4	h6
32	♖g3	♔h7
33	♖h5	♖c1+
34	♔h2	♖b1
35	♘g5+	♔g8
36	♘e4	♖1xb3
37	f3	f5
38	♘c5	♗d6
39	♘xb3	♖xb3
40	f4	♗xf4
	White resigns	

	Game 39 **Tiviakov–Dreev** *Podolsk 1992*	
1	e4	e6
2	d4	d5
3	♘d2	c5
4	exd5	♕xd5
5	♘gf3	cxd4
6	♗c4	♕d6
7	0-0	♘f6
8	♘b3	♘c6
9	♘bxd4	♘xd4
10	♘xd4	a6
11	b3	♕c7
12	♗b2	♗d6
13	h3	0-0
14	a4?!	

22 ... ♕xb5!

The former World Champion increases his advantage by going into the endgame. 22...♕a7 is less clear on account of 23 b4.

23 ♗xb5 ♘e4
24 ♗e2 ♗d5!
25 ♗f3 ♘f6

An impulsive move; 25...f6 was stronger.

26 ♗xd5 ♘xd5
27 ♘f5?

An 'eternal' centralised knight is often not inferior in strength to a rook, and, had White sensed the danger, he would have found the counter resource 27 ♘b5! After the pseudo-active move played, Black intensifies the pressure.

27 ... ♗f8
28 ♘g3

28 ♘e3 cuts off the rook – 28...♗d6! 29 ♖g5 f6!, but now comes the turn of the weak b3 pawn.

28 ... ♖d6!

This move prevents ...b7-b5, but Black can switch to play in the centre. In this respect 14 ♕f3 is more versatile, when 14...e5 is not good on account of 15 ♘f5, eyeing not only the bishop at d6, but also the h6 square (15...e4?? 16 ♘h6+ ♔h8 17 ♕xf6! and wins).

14	...	e5
15	♘f3	e4!
16	♘d4	

The initiative is already with Black. To 16 ♘g5 ♗e5 17 ♗a3 he has the reply 17...b5!

| 16 | ... | ♗d7 |
| 17 | ♕e2 | ♖ae8! |

The foresight of moving this rook is revealed within a few moves, but for the moment Black threatens the breakthrough 18...e3! 19 fxe3 ♗h2+ 20 ♔h1 ♘e4.

| 18 | ♗c1 | ♕a5 |

The queen is to be transferred to e5, but the shorter route 18...♕c5?! is ruled out – 19 ♗a3! ♕xd4 20 ♖fd1.

| 19 | ♖d1 | ♕e5 |
| 20 | g3 | ♘h5 |

Not 20...♗xh3? on account of 21 ♗f4 ♕c5 22 ♗xd6 ♕xd6 23 ♘e6!

| 21 | ♕f1 | ♗c5 |
| 22 | c3 | ♔h8! |

The final reserves come into play.

23	♕g2	f5
24	♘e2	♗c6
25	♗f4	

White somehow has to 'plug the holes'.

25	...	♘xf4
26	gxf4	♕c7
27	♗d5	♖f6
28	♔h1	♖g6
29	♕f1	♗d6
30	♗xc6	♕xc6

After 30...bxc6 White could have activated his game by 31 ♘d4 ♗xf4 32 ♕xa6.

| 31 | c4 | ♕b6 |
| 32 | ♖d5 | |

After 32 ♖ab1 ♗c5 the f2 pawn is lost (33 f3? ♕c6).

| 32 | ... | ♕xb3 |
| 33 | ♘d4 | ♕c3?! |

It would have been better to retain the queen by retreating it to b6, but Black overestimates the role of the passed d-pawn that he now creates, although, fortunately, it eventually wins him the game.

34	♖c1	♕d3
35	♕xd3	exd3
36	♖d1	d2!
37	♘f3	♗xf4
38	♖xf5?	

White has parried the mating threats, but he cannot resist the temptation of picking up (with gain of tempo!) the f5 pawn, thinking that the d2 pawn will not run away. But he has clearly underestimated the threats on the f-file.

| 38 | ... | ♖f6 |
| 39 | ♖d5 | h6 |

40	♘xd2	♖e2
41	♔g1	♗g5
42	f3	♗e3+
43	♔h1	

After 43 ♔f1 White suffers a linear mate: 43...♖f2+ 44 ♔e1 ♖g6.

43	...	♖g6
44	♖d3	♗f4
45	♘f1	♖eg2!

White resigns

Game 40
Timoshchenko–Danielian
Cappelle la Grande 1994

1	e4	e6
2	d4	d5
3	♘d2	c5
4	exd5	♕xd5
5	♘gf3	cxd4
6	♗c4	♕d6
7	0-0	♘f6
8	♘b3	♘c6
9	♘bxd4	♘xd4
10	♘xd4	a6
11	b3	♕c7
12	♗b2	♗d6
13	♘f3	b6
14	♖e1	

Against the plan chosen by Black of developing his queenside, White can consider 14 ♕e2!? ♗b7 15 a4, preventing queenside castling and intending an invasion at e5.

| 14 | ... | ♗b7 |
| 15 | ♗d3 | ♘d5! |

A typical manoeuvre: the knight sets its sights on the f4 square.

| 16 | a4 | 0-0-0 |
| 17 | g3 | ♔b8 |

18 ♗xg7?

A risky move. In his calculations White apparently overlooked Black's 21st move. He should have limited himself to 18 ♕e2 ♘b4 (18...♔a7 is not good on account of 19 a5±) 19 ♗e4 ♗xe4 20 ♕xe4 ♕xc2 21 ♗xg7 ♖hg8 22 ♗e5, maintaining the balance.

18	...	♖hg8
19	♗e5	♗xe5
20	♘xe5	f6
21	♘c4	♘c3!

Now White has no defence against the attack on the long a8-h1 diagonal.

22	♕h5	♕c6
23	f3	♖g5
24	♕h3	♖xd3!

Eliminating a potential defender (24...♕xf3 25 ♗f1).

| 25 | cxd3 | ♕xf3 |

26 ♘d6 ♖h5 27 ♕f1 ♕h1+ 28 ♔f2 ♕f3+ 29 ♔g1 ♕h1+ 30 ♔f2 ♕xh2+ 31 ♔e3 ♖e5+ 32 ♘e4 ♘d5+ **White resigns**

18   10...a6 11 ♗b3

1	e4	e6
2	d4	d5
3	♘d2	c5
4	exd5	♕xd5
5	♘gf3	cxd4
6	♗c4	♕d6
7	0-0	♘f6
8	♘b3	♘c6
9	♘bxd4	♘xd4
10	♘xd4	a6
11	♗b3	

A prophylactic bishop retreat. Now after the black queen moves to c7 White can develop his queen at f3, preventing ...b7-b5. However, the loss of a tempo broadens the options for Black, who, apart from the usual setting up of a battery on the b8-h2 diagonal, can also aim for sharper play with queenside castling.

Therefore his main continuations are **11...♗d7 (18.1)** and **11...♕c7 (18.2)**.

In view of the tempo lost (...a7-a6), the more passive plan with 11...♗e7 often leads to difficulties. For example: 12 c3 0-0 13 ♕f3 ♕c7 14 ♗g5 (14 h3 b5? 15 ♕xa8 ♗b7 16 ♕a7 e5 17 ♘e6±, Popovic-Reefat, Moscow Olympiad 1994; 14 ♖e1 ♗d6 15 h3 e5!?∞) 14...♗d7 15 ♖fe1± (Jansa-Petrosian, Moscow 1977).

18.1

(1 e4 e6 2 d4 d5 3 ♘d2 c5 4 exd5 ♕xd5 5 ♘gf3 cxd4 6 ♗c4 ♕d6 7 0-0 ♘f6 8 ♘b3 ♘c6 9 ♘bxd4 ♘xd4 10 ♘xd4 a6 11 ♗b3)

11 ...   ♗d7

12 c3   ♛c7

12...0-0-0 13 ♛f3 e5 (13...♛c7 14 ♗f4±) 14 ♘f5±.

13 ♗g5

13 ♛f3 ♗d6 14 h3 ♗h2+ 15 ♔h1 ♗e5 16 ♖e1 0-0 17 ♗e3± (Campora-Bielicki, Buenos Aires 1989).

13 ...   ♘e4

(a) 13...0-0-0 14 ♗xf6 gxf6 15 ♛h5 ♗e8 16 ♖ad1±;

(b) 13...♗d6!? 14 ♗xf6 gxf6 15 ♛h5 ♛c5! 16 ♛f3 ♛e5 17 g3 0-0-0 18 ♖fe1 ♛g5 19 ♗c4± (Ivanchuk).

14 ♗h4!

14 ♗e3 ♘f6!

14 ...   ♗d6

14...♛f4? 15 g3! ♛h6 16 ♛e2 ♘d6 17 f4± (17 ♛e5±) (Ivanchuk-Glek, USSR 1988) – *Game 41*.

15 ♛g4

15 ♛e2 ♘c5 16 ♘f5 ♗xh2+ 17 ♔h1 0-0 18 ♘xg7!± (Wahls-Lautier, Biel 1990).

15	**...**	**♗xh2+**
16	**♔h1**	**♛f4**
17	**♛xg7**	**♛xh4**
18	**♛xh8+**	**♔e7**
19	**♘f3**	**♛h5**
20	**♛xa8**	**♗c7+**
21	**♔g1**	

Tairi-Akvist (Sweden 1990).

21	**...**	**♘g5!?**
22	**♖fd1**	**♗c6±**

18.2

(1 e4 e6 2 d4 d5 3 ♘d2 c5 4 exd5 ♛xd5 5 ♘gf3 cxd4 6 ♗c4 ♛d6 7 0-0 ♘f6 8 ♘b3 ♘c6 9 ♘bxd4 ♘xd4 10 ♘xd4 a6 11 ♗b3)

11 ...   ♛c7

12 ♛f3

(a) 12 ♛e2 ♗e7 13 ♗g5 0-0 14 ♖ad1 ♘d5 15 ♗c1 ♗f6 16 ♖fe1 ♗d7= (Hracek-Chernin, Moscow Olympiad 1994);

(b) 12 ♖e1 – 11 ♖e1 (section 19.1).

12 ...   ♗d6

13 h3

13 ♔h1 0-0 14 ♗g5 ♘d7 15 c3 ♘e5! 16 ♛h5 ♘g6 17 ♗c2 h6 (17...♛c5 18 ♛g4 ♗d7=, Svidler-Ionov, St Petersburg 1996) 18 ♘f3∞ (Ivanchuk-Anand, Reggio Emilia 1991/2) – *Game 42*.

13 ...   0-0

14 ♗g5   ♘d7

14...♗h2+ 15 ♔h1 ♗e5 16 ♖ad1 b6 17 ♗xf6 ♗xf6 18 ♛xa8± (Yakovich-Eingorn, Kharkov 1985).

15 c3

15 ♖ad1 ♘c5=.

15 ...   b5

15...♘e5 16 ♛h5 ♘g6 17 ♗c2 h6 18 ♗e3 ♘f4 19 ♛h4 ♘d5 20

♗d2 b5 21 ♖ae1 ♖b8 22 ♗h6± (Isupov-Hoang, Budapest 1994).

16 ♖ad1   ♗b7

16...♘c5 17 ♗c2 ♗b7 18 ♕h5 (18 ♕g4!?) 18...♗e4= (Hellers-Hübner, Wijk aan Zee 1986).

17 ♕g4

17 ...   ♘c5!

(a) 17...♘e5? 18 ♘xe6!±;

(b) 17...♗h2+? 18 ♔h1 ♘e5 19 ♘xe6!± (A.Sokolov-Nogueiras, Clermont-Ferrand 1989) – *Game 43*;

(c) 17...♔h8 18 ♕h4 (18 ♖fe1 ♘e5 19 ♕h5 ♘g6 20 ♗c2 ♔g8 21 ♘f3 ♗xf3 22 ♕xf3±, Hübner-Korchnoi, Brussels 1986) 18...♖ae8?! (18...♖fe8 △ ...♘f8±) 19 ♖fe1 ♘c5 20 ♗c2 f5 21 ♘xf5!± (Marciano-Touzane, France 1991).

18 ♗f6   g6
19 ♖fe1   ♘xb3
20 axb3   ♖fe8
21 ♖d3   ♗h2+
22 ♔h1   ♕f4=

Adams-Levitt (London 1989).

Game 41
Ivanchuk–Glek
Frunze 1988

1	e4	e6
2	d4	d5
3	♘d2	c5
4	exd5	♕xd5
5	♘gf3	cxd4
6	♗c4	♕d6
7	0-0	♘f6
8	♘b3	♘c6
9	♘bxd4	♘xd4
10	♘xd4	a6
11	♗b3	♗d7
12	c3	♕c7
13	♗g5	♘e4
14	♗h4!	♕f4
15	g3!	

Initiating complications, since now the bishop at h4 is in danger. White cannot achieve anything real from the opening of the f-file after 15 ♗g3 ♘xg3 16 fxg3 ♕e3+ 17 ♔h1 ♗e7, for example 18 ♖xf7?! ♔xf7 19 ♘f5 ♕g5 20 ♕xd7 ♕xf5 21 ♖e1 ♔f8! 22 g4 ♕f4!, and 23 ♕xe6? fails to 23...♗d6! (Ivanchuk).

15 ...   ♕h6
16 ♕e2   ♘d6
17 f4

17 ♕e5! is stronger, when 17...f6? loses to 18 ♘xe6! fxe5 19 ♘c7 mate.

17 ...   ♘b5
18 ♘f5   ♗c5+?

Ivanchuk considers that the only way to resist was by 18...♕g6 19 ♗c2 f6! 20 ♘d6+ ♘xd6 21 ♗xg6+ hxg6, when although Black has only two pieces for the queen, after ...♘f5 they will display their strength, while at the same time the bishop at h4 is out of play. But now this manoeuvre does not work, since the bishop at c5 is unprotected.

| 19 | ♔g2 | ♕g6 |
| 20 | ♗c2 | f6 |

After 20...♗c6+ 21 ♔h3 ♔f8 22 ♘d4! the bishop at c6 is exchanged, and White retains his advantage.

21	♘xg7+!	♕xg7
22	♕h5+	♕f7
23	♕xc5	♖c8
24	♕e3	0-0
25	♖ad1	♗c6+
26	♔g1	♗d5
27	f5	♖c6
28	♗xf6!	♕xf6
29	fxe6	♖xe6
30	♕d3	♕h6
31	♕xd5	♕e3+
32	♔h1	♖xf1+
33	♖xf1	♘d6
34	♗b3	

Black resigns

Game 42
Ivanchuk–Anand
Reggio Emilia 1991/2

1	d4	e6
2	e4	d5
3	♘d2	c5
4	exd5	♕xd5
5	♘gf3	cxd4
6	♗c4	♕d6
7	0-0	♘f6
8	♘b3	♘c6
9	♘bxd4	♘xd4
10	♘xd4	a6
11	♗b3	♕c7
12	♕f3	♗d6
13	♔h1	0-0
14	♗g5	♘d7
15	c3	♘e5!

After 15...b5? 16 ♖ad1 ♘c5 17 ♗c2 ♗b7 18 ♕h3! Black comes under an attack.

| 16 | ♕h5 | ♘g6 |

| 17 | ♗c2 | |

After 17 ♖ad1 Black exchanges the important bishop by 17...♗f4!

17 ...   h6

An alternative is 17...♛c5 18 ♛g4 ♗d7= (Svidler-Ionov, St Petersburg 1996).

18 ♘f3

To 18 ♗e3 Black has the good reply 18...♘f4 19 ♛h4 ♗d7!

18 ...   b5!?

18...♘f4 19 ♛h4 ♘g6 is also possible.

19 ♖ad1   ♗f4!
20 ♗xf4

White simplifies the position, since in the event of 20 ♗xg6 ♗xg5 21 ♗e4 g6! 22 ♛h3 e5 Black seizes the initiative.

20	...	♘xf4
21	♛e5	♛xe5
22	♘xe5	♗b7
23	f3	♖fd8
24	♔g1	♖ac8
25	a3	f6
26	♘d3	♘xd3
27	♖xd3	♖xd3
28	♗xd3	♖d8
29	♖d1	♔f8
30	♗e2	♖xd1+
31	♗xd1	g5
32	g3	♔e7
33	♔f2	a5
34	f4?!	

By playing 34 ♔e3! ♔d6 35 f4 gxf4+ 36 ♔xf4! White would have retained a slight advantage in the endgame.

34	...	gxf4
35	gxf4	♔d6
36	b4	axb4
37	cxb4?	

37 axb4 was essential, retaining the possibility of creating a passed pawn. Now a draw is inevitable.

37	...	e5
38	♔e3	♗c6
39	♗h5	♗d7
40	♗f7	♗c6
41	h4	♔e7
42	♗b3	♔d6
43	♗d1	f5
44	♗c2	♗d7
	draw agreed	

Game 43
A.Sokolov–Nogueiras
Clermont-Ferrand 1989

1	e4	e6
2	d4	d5
3	♘d2	c5
4	exd5	♛xd5
5	♘gf3	cxd4
6	♗c4	♛d6
7	0-0	♘f6
8	♘b3	♘c6
9	♘bxd4	♘xd4
10	♘xd4	a6
11	♗b3	♛c7
12	♛f3	♗d6
13	h3	0-0
14	♗g5	♘d7
15	c3	b5
16	♖ad1	♗b7
17	♛g4	♗h2+?!

A poor manoeuvre – Black overlooks White's 19th move. 17...♘c5 is more natural and stronger.

18 ♔h1   ♘e5

19	♘xe6!	fxe6
20	♕xe6+	♔h8
21	f4	♖fe8

21...♖ae8? can be met by 22 fxe5.

22	♕d6	♕xd6
23	♖xd6	♗g3?

It was essential to go into the ending with opposite-colour bishops by 23...♘c4 24 ♗xc4 bxc4 25 ♖b6 ♗d5 26 ♔xh2 ♖e2, when the activity of Black's pieces compensates for his material deficit.

24	fxe5	♖xe5
25	♖d8+	♖xd8
26	♗xd8	h5
27	♗d1	♖d5
28	♖f8+	♔h7
29	♗c2+	g6
30	♗f6	

Black resigns

19   10...a6 11 ♖e1

1	e4	e6
2	d4	d5
3	♘d2	c5
4	exd5	♕xd5
5	♘gf3	cxd4
6	♗c4	♕d6
7	0-0	♘f6
8	♘b3	♘c6
9	♘bxd4	♘xd4
10	♘xd4	a6
11	♖e1	

One of the most critical continuations. In anticipation of Black setting up his dark-square battery on the b8-h2 diagonal, White exploits the delay in castling to switch his knight to the kingside, for which he is prepared to sacrifice his h2 pawn. Here too Black can choose the plan with queenside castling, and therefore his main continuations are **11...♕c7 (19.1)** and **11...♗d7 (19.2)**.

19.1

(1 e4 e6 2 d4 d5 3 ♘d2 c5 4 exd5 ♕xd5 5 ♘gf3 cxd4 6 ♗c4 ♕d6 7 0-0 ♘f6 8 ♘b3 ♘c6 9 ♘bxd4 ♘xd4 10 ♘xd4 a6 11 ♖e1)

    11   ...   ♕c7

    12 ♗b3

(a) 12 ♗d3:

(a1) 12...♗d6 13 ♘f5?! ♗xh2+ 14 ♔h1 ♔f8! (14...h5 15 g3 ♔f8 [15...h4 16 ♗f4 ♕c6+ 17 ♔xh2 hxg3+ 18 ♔xg3 ♘h5+? 19 ♕xh5±] 16 ♗f4 ♕b6 [16...♕c6+ 17 ♗e4!±] 17 ♗d6+ ♔e8 18 ♘xg7+ ♔d7 19 ♗e5±, Shamkovich-Seirawan, USA Ch 1980) 15 g3 exf5 16 ♔xh2 h5→ (Smagin-Akopian, Yerevan 1988) – *Game 44*;

(a2) 12...♗c5 13 c3 0-0 14 ♗g5 ♗xd4 15 cxd4 ♘d5 16 ♖c1 ♕d6 17

♕h5 f5= (Frolov-Soffer, Berlin 1993);

(b) 12 ♕e2:

(b1) 12...♗c5 13 c3 0-0 (13...b5 14 ♗d3 ♗xd4 15 cxd4 0-0 16 ♗g5 ♘d5 17 ♖ac1 ♕d6 18 ♕h5→, Adams-Levitt, Preston 1989) 14 ♗g5 ♗xd4 15 cxd4 ♘d5 16 ♗xd5 (16 ♖ac1 ♕d6 17 ♕f3 f6!? 18 ♗d2 ♖d8=) 16...exd5 17 ♗e7 ♖e8 18 ♗d8 ♖xe2 19 ♗xc7 ♖xe1+ 20 ♖xe1 ♗e6 ½-½ (Tal-Korchnoi, Brussels 1988);

(b2) 12...♗d6 13 ♗g5 0-0 14 g3 ♘e4= (Van der Wiel-Nogueiras, Rotterdam 1989);

(c) 12 b3 ♗d6 13 h3 0-0 14 ♗b2 b5 15 ♗d3 ♗b7 16 ♘f3 ♖ad8 17 ♕e2 ♕c6 18 ♕e3 ♗e7 19 ♖ad1 h6 20 ♕f4 ♘h5 21 ♕g4 ♘f6= (Xie Jun-Gulko, San Francisco 1995).

12...♗d6 (19.11)
12...♗d7 (19.12)

19.11

(1 e4 e6 2 d4 d5 3 ♘d2 c5 4 exd5 ♕xd5 5 ♘gf3 cxd4 6 ♗c4 ♕d6 7 0-0 ♘f6 8 ♘b3 ♘c6 9 ♘bxd4 ♘xd4 10 ♘xd4 a6 11 ♖e1 ♕c7 12 ♗b3)

12 ...   ♗d6

13 ♘f5

(a) 13 h3 0-0 14 ♗g5 b5 (14... ♘d7? 15 ♖xe6!±±, Adams-Luther, Oakham 1990):

(a1) 15 ♗xf6 gxf6 16 ♕h5 ♗b7 17 c3 ♔h8 18 ♕h6 ♖g8!? 19 ♕xf6+ ♖g7 20 f3 ♖ag8∞ (Jansa-Brunner, Bad Wörishofen 1989);

(a2) 15 c3 – 11 c3 ♕c7 12 ♗b3 ♗d6 13 h3 0-0 14 ♖e1 b5 15 ♗g5 (section 16.1);

(b) 13 g3 0-0 14 ♗g5 b5 (14...♗e5!?∞) 15 ♗xf6 gxf6 16 ♕d2 ♗e5 17 c3± (A.Ivanov-Brunner, Gausdal 1991).

13 ...   ♗xh2+
14 ♔h1

14...♔f8 (19.111)
14...0-0 (19.112)

19.111

(1 e4 e6 2 d4 d5 3 ♘d2 c5 4 exd5
♕xd5 5 ♘gf3 cxd4 6 ♗c4 ♕d6 7
0-0 ♘f6 8 ♘b3 ♘c6 9 ♘bxd4
♘xd4 10 ♘xd4 a6 11 ♖e1 ♕c7 12
♗b3 ♗d6 13 ♘f5 ♗xh2+ 14 ♔h1)

14   ...   ♔f8

15   ♕d4
15 g3:
   (a) 15...♗xg3?! 16 ♘xg3 b5 17
♔g2± (Psakhis-Speelman, Moscow
1990) – *Game 45*;
   (a) 15...exf5 16 ♗f4 ♕c6+ (16...
♕b6?! 17 ♕d6+ ♕xd6 18 ♗xd6+
♔g8 19 ♖e7±, Himmel-Andersen,
Dortmund 1993) 17 ♔xh2 ♗e6 18
♗d6+ (18 ♕d6+ ♕xd6 19 ♗xd6+
♔e8 20 ♖ad1 ♘e4 21 f3 ♘xd6 22
♖xd6 ♖c8 23 ♖b6 ♖c7 24 ♗xe6
fxe6 25 ♖exe6+ ♔f7=, Psakhis-
Pomes, Groningen 1991) 18...♔e8

19 c4 (19 ♕d4 ♖d8 20 ♖ad1±,
Jansa-Hübner,   Germany   1991)
19...h5 (19...♘e4 20 c5±, Mannion-
S.Lalic, Newcastle 1996) 20 c5 h4
21 f3 ♔d8 22 ♗xe6± (Adams-
Pomes, Terrassa 1991).
   15 ...   h6
   (a) 15...exf5 16 ♕xf6! h6
(16...♗e6 17 ♗h6!) 17 ♕d4 ♗d6
18 ♖d1±;
   (b) 15...h5 16 ♗g5 ♘e8 17
♗d8!± (Pandavos-Skalkotas, Athens
1991).
      16 g3
   16 ♗d2 exf5 17 ♗b4+ ♔g8 18
♖e7 ♕f4 19 ♗c3 ♗e6 20 ♗xe6
♕xd4 21 ♗xd4 fxe6 22 ♔xh2 e5=
(Müller-Hertneck, Germany 1991).
      16 ...   exf5
      17   ♗f4   ♕c6+
      18   ♔xh2   ♔g8
18...♗e6 19 ♗d6+ ♔g8 20
♖xe6!±±.
      19   ♖e7±
Belyavsky-Hertneck   (Munich
1991).

19.112

(1 e4 e6 2 d4 d5 3 ♘d2 c5 4 exd5
♕xd5 5 ♘gf3 cxd4 6 ♗c4 ♕d6 7
0-0 ♘f6 8 ♘b3 ♘c6 9 ♘bxd4
♘xd4 10 ♘xd4 a6 11 ♖e1 ♕c7 12
♗b3 ♗d6 13 ♘f5 ♗xh2+ 14 ♔h1)

      14   ...   0-0
      15   ♘xg7   ♖d8
15...♔xg7:
   (a) 16 ♕d4 ♗d6 (16...e5?! 17
♕h4 ♘g4 18 f3!±,   Geenen-

Vangeldorp, Belgium 1990 – *Game 46*) 17 ♗h6+ ♔g6 18 c3 (18 ♕h4 ♕c5! △ ...♕h5) 18...♘h5 19 ♗xf8 ♗xf8 20 ℤe5 f5 21 g4 ♕c6+ 22 ♔h2 ♘f6∞ (Brunell-Wiedenkeller, Stockholm 1990);

(b) 16 ♕d2!? ♘g8 17 ♕g5+ ♔h8 18 f4 f6 19 ♕h4 ♗xf4 20 ♗xf4 e5 21 ♗xg8 ♔xg8 22 ♗h6 ℤf7 23 ℤad1≡↑ (Chernin).

16 ♕e2 (19.1121)
16 ♕f3 (19.1122)

16 ♘h5 ℤxd1 17 ♘xf6+ ♔h8 18 ℤxd1 ♗e5 19 ♗g5 ♕e7∓ (S.Ivanov).

> **19.1121**

(1 e4 e6 2 d4 d5 3 ♘d2 c5 4 exd5 ♕xd5 5 ♘gf3 cxd4 6 ♗c4 ♕d6 7 0-0 ♘f6 8 ♘b3 ♘c6 9 ♘bxd4 ♘xd4 10 ♘xd4 a6 11 ℤe1 ♕c7 12 ♗b3 ♗d6 13 ♘f5 ♗xh2+ 14 ♔h1 0-0 15 ♘xg7 ℤd8)

16 ♕e2

16 ... ♔xg7
17 g3 ♗xg3
18 fxg3

18 ℤg1!? ♕c6+ 19 f3 ♕c7∓.

18 ... ♕c5

(a) 18...b5? 19 ♗f4 ♗b7+ 20 ♔h2 ♕c5 21 ♗e5 ♔g6 22 ♗xf6 ♔xf6 23 ℤf1+! ♔g6 24 ♗xe6± (Adams-Dreev, Debrecen 1992);

(b) 18...♕c6+ 19 ♔h2 h5 20 ♕e5 ♕f3∞ (Mannion-Bryson, Scotland 1993).

19 ♗f4! ♕h5+

19...♗d7!? 20 ♗e5 ♗c6+ 21 ♔h2 ♔g6 (△ 22...♕xe5) 22 ♗xf6 ♔xf6 23 ℤf1+ ♔g6 24 ♗xe6 ♕h5+ 25 ♕xh5+ ♔xh5 26 ♗xf7+ ♔g5≡ (Dreev).

20 ♕xh5 ♘xh5
21 ♗c7 ℤd7
22 ♗e5+ f6

22...♔g6 23 ℤf1≡.

23 g4 fxe5 24 gxh5 b5= Vorontsov-Savchenko (St Petersburg 1993).

19.1122

(1 e4 e6 2 d4 d5 3 ♘d2 c5 4 exd5 ♕xd5 5 ♘gf3 cxd4 6 ♗c4 ♕d6 7 0-0 ♘f6 8 ♘b3 ♘c6 9 ♘bxd4 ♘xd4 10 ♘xd4 a6 11 ♖e1 ♕c7 12 ♗b3 ♗d6 13 ♘f5 ♗xh2+ 14 ♔h1 0-0 15 ♘xg7 ♖d8)

16   ♕f3

16   ...   ♔xg7
17   ♗h6+

17 g3?! b5:

(a) 18 ♗f4?! ♗b7 19 ♗xc7 ♗xf3+ 20 ♔xh2 ♘g4+ 21 ♔g1 ♖d2 22 ♖f1 ♖c8 23 ♗b6 (23 ♗a5? ♖c5!∓∓, Ye Jiangchuan-Dolmatov, Moscow 1992) 23...e5∓;

(b) 18 ♔xh2 ♗b7 19 ♕e2 (19 ♕f4 ♕c6! 20 ♖g1 ♖d1!∓, Wolff-Gulko, USA Ch 1992 – *Game 47*) 19...♕c6 (19...♖d4!? 20 f4 ♖ad8↑, S.Ivanov) 20 ♖g1 ♖ac8 21 ♕e5 (21 ♗g5? ♕c5∓, Yandemirov-S.Ivanov, Minsk 1995) 21...♕c5 22 ♕xc5 ♖xc5 23 g4!∞ (S.Ivanov).

17   ...   ♔g6
18   c3

18 c4?! ♘h5! 19 ♗e3 f5 20 g4 ♘f6∓ (Gufeld-Ravi, Calcutta 1994) – *Game 48*.

18   ...   ♘h5!?

(a) 18...♗e5 19 ♕e3±±;

(b) 18...♖d5 19 ♗c2+ ♖f5 20 ♕e3±±;

(c) 18...e5 19 ♗c2+ e4 20 ♗xe4+ ♘xe4 21 ♖xe4 Δ 22 ♖h4±± (Adams);

(d) 18...♘d5:

(d1) 19 ♖e4 ♔xh6 20 ♖g4 ♘f4 21 g3 ♖d3= (Khalifman-Gulko, Lucerne 1993);

(d2) 19 g3 ♔xh6 20 ♗xd5 ♔g7 21 ♗e4 f5 22 ♔xh2 fxe4 23 ♖xe4 e5 24 ♖ae1 ♖e8 25 ♕h5 ♕f7∓ (Gulko);

(d3) 19 ♗c1 f5!? (19...♗f4 20 ♗xd5! ♗xc1 21 ♗e4+ f5 22 ♖axc1 fxe4 23 ♖xe4 ♖d5 24 ♖g4+ ♖g5 25 ♖xg5+ ♔xg5 26 ♖d1!∞→, Berelovich-Savchenko, Groningen 1993) 20 g3 ♘f6 21 ♗xe6 ♗xe6 22 ♖xe6

♗xg3 23 fxg3 ♕c4! 24 ♖e1 ♖d3∓
(Holmes-Grant, Scottish Ch 1994);

   (d4) 19 ♖ad1! (Speelman) 19...
f5 20 ♗c1 ♗d6 21 ♗xd5 exd5 22
♖xd5±±→ (Adams-Dreev, Wijk aan
Zee 1996) – *Game 49*.

    19 ♖e4

   19 ♗e3 (Gulko) 19...f5 20 g4
♘f6∞.

    19 ... ♔xh6
    20 ♖h4 ♕e5!∞
(Khalifman).

    21 ♗c2 ♗f4
    22 g4 ♔g7
    **23 ♖xh5 ♕f6 24 g5 ♗xg5 25
♖xg5+ ♕xg5 26 ♖g1 ♖d5∞**
(Thomas-DeMauro, corr. 1996).

19.12

(1 e4 e6 2 d4 d5 3 ♘d2 c5 4 exd5
♕xd5 5 ♘gf3 cxd4 6 ♗c4 ♕d6 7
0-0 ♘f6 8 ♘b3 ♘c6 9 ♘bxd4
♘xd4 10 ♘xd4 a6 11 ♖e1 ♕c7 12
♗b3)

    12 ... ♗d7

    13 ♕f3
   (a) 13 ♕e2 ♗d6 14 h3 0-0-0 15
c3 ♖hg8 16 a4 g5∓ (Csoke-Hoang,
Budapest 1994);
   (b) 13 ♗g5!? ♗c5 (13...♗d6!?)
14 c3 0-0-0 15 ♕f3±.

    13 ... ♗d6
    14 h3
   (a) 14 ♘f5? ♗xh2+ 15 ♔h1
0-0-0! 16 ♘xg7 ♗e5 17 ♕e2 ♗d4!
18 c3 ♗b5 19 ♕f3 ♗c6∓ (I.Gure-
vich-Akopian, Aguadilla 1989);
   (b) 14 ♗xe6 fxe6 15 ♘xe6
♗xe6 16 ♖xe6+ ♔f7 17 ♕b3
♗xh2+ 18 ♔h1 ♔g6 19 ♕d3+ ♔f7
20 ♕b3 ♔g6= (Belikov-Danielian,
Yurmala 1991).

    14 ... 0-0-0
    15 ♗g5
   15 a4 ♔b8 16 ♗g5! ♖hg8
(16...e5!? 17 ♘f5 e4 18 ♖xe4 ♘xe4
19 ♗xd8 ♗h2+! 20 ♔h1 ♘xf2+ 21
♕xf2 ♖xd8∞, L.B.Hansen) 17 ♖ad1
♔a8 18 ♔h1 h6 19 ♗xf6 (19 ♗h4
♗f4 △ 20...g5) 19...gxf6 20 ♕xf6
♖df8⩱ (Berg-L.B.Hansen, Danish
Ch 1994).

    15 ... ♕c5
   15...♗h2+ 16 ♔h1 ♗e5 17 ♕e3
♗xd4 18 ♕xd4 ♗c6= (Akopian).

    16 ♗e3 ♕e5
    17 g3 ♕e4
    18 ♖ad1 ♗c6
    19 ♕xe4 ♗xe4
    20 ♗g5 ♗g6
    21 c3 h6
   21...♗c5= (Tiviakov-Kramnik,
USSR Ch 1991).

    22 ♗xf6 gxf6
    23 ♗c2 ♗xc2

24 ♘xc2 f5=
Rozentalis-L.B.Hansen (Malmo 1993).

19.2

(1 e4 e6 2 d4 d5 3 ♘d2 c5 4 exd5 ♕xd5 5 ♘gf3 cxd4 6 ♗c4 ♕d6 7 0-0 ♘f6 8 ♘b3 ♘c6 9 ♘bxd4 ♘xd4 10 ♘xd4 a6 11 ♖e1)

11 ... ♗d7

12 h3 (19.21)
12 ♗b3 (19.22)
12 c3 (19.23)

12 ♗g5 · 0-0-0 (12...♕c5? 13 ♗xe6! fxe6 14 ♗xf6 gxf6 15 ♘xe6 ♗xe6 16 ♖xe6+ ♗e7 17 b4! ♕xb4 18 ♕h5+ ♔f8 19 ♖ae1 ♖e8 20 g3±, Vaisser) 13 ♗b3 ♕c7 14 ♕f3 ♗d6 15 h3 ♕c5 16 ♕e3 (16 ♗xf6?! gxf6 17 ♕xf6 ♖hg8 18 ♖ad1 ♖g6 19 ♕xf7 ♕g5 20 g4 ♖f8 21 ♕xh7 ♕f4∓, Vaisser) 16...♕c7= (Relange-Danielian, Cannes 1993).

19.21

(1 e4 e6 2 d4 d5 3 ♘d2 c5 4 exd5 ♕xd5 5 ♘gf3 cxd4 6 ♗c4 ♕d6 7 0-0 ♘f6 8 ♘b3 ♘c6 9 ♘bxd4 ♘xd4 10 ♘xd4 a6 11 ♖e1 ♗d7)

12 h3

12 ... 0-0-0
13 c3 ♕c7
14 ♕e2 ♗c5
14...♗d6 15 ♘f3 (15 a4?! e5 16 ♘c2 ♗f5 17 ♘e3 ♗g6 18 b4 e4 19 ♗a3 ♗h2+ 20 ♔h1 ♗f4∓, Xie Jun-Smyslov, Vienna 1993) 15...♗c6 16 ♘e5∞.
15 ♗e3
15 b4 ♗a7 16 b5 e5 (16...♗b8!? 17 ♘f3 axb5 18 ♗xb5 e5!∞, Smagin) 17 ♘c2 axb5 18 ♗xb5 ♗xf2+ 19 ♔xf2 ♕b6+= (A.Sokolov-Hübner, Tilburg 1987).
15 ... e5
16 ♘c2 ♗xe3
17 ♘xe3 ♗c6 18 ♖ad1±
(Smagin-Luther, Germany 1992).

| 19.22 |

(1 e4 e6 2 d4 d5 3 ♘d2 c5 4 exd5
♕xd5 5 ♘gf3 cxd4 6 ♗c4 ♕d6 7
0-0 ♘f6 8 ♘b3 ♘c6 9 ♘bxd4
♘xd4 10 ♘xd4 a6 11 ♖e1 ♗d7)

12   ♗b3

12   ...   0-0-0
12...♕c7 – 11...♕c7 12 ♗b3
♗d7 (section 19.12).
    13   ♗g5
13 c3 ♕c7 14 ♕e2 ♗d6 15 h3
♔b8 16 ♗g5 h6 17 ♗h4 ♖hf8=
(Zapata-Ivanchuk, Manila Interzonal 1990).
    13   ...   ♕c7
13...h6 14 ♗h4 ♕c7 15 ♗g3
♗d6 16 ♗xd6 ♕xd6 17 ♘f3 ♕f4
(Pandavos-Djurhuus, Haifa 1989)
18 ♘e5±.
    14   ♕f3
14 c3 ♗d6 15 ♗xf6 gxf6
(15...♗xh2+ 16 ♔h1 gxf6 17 ♕h5
♗e5 18 ♕xf7 △ 18...♖df8 19
♘xe6!→, Kramnik) 16 ♕h5 ♖df8

17 g3 ♕c5= (Kotronias-Kramnik,
Chalkidiki 1992) – *Game 50*.
14	...	♗d6
15	h3	♗h2+
16	♔h1	♗e5
17	♖ad1	♗xd4
18	♖xd4	♗c6
19	♕c3	♖xd4
20	♕xd4	♖d8
21	♕h4	
21 ♕a7 ♕a5!=; 21 ♕c4!?
21	...	♕a5!
22	c3	♕f5=
Wolff-Mednis (New York 1990).

| 19.23 |

(1 e4 e6 2 d4 d5 3 ♘d2 c5 4 exd5
♕xd5 5 ♘gf3 cxd4 6 ♗c4 ♕d6 7
0-0 ♘f6 8 ♘b3 ♘c6 9 ♘bxd4
♘xd4 10 ♘xd4 a6 11 ♖e1 ♗d7)

12   c3

12   ...   ♕c7

13 ♗b3 (19.231)
13 ♕e2 (19.232)

19.231

(1 e4 e6 2 d4 d5 3 ♘d2 c5 4 exd5 ♕xd5 5 ♘gf3 cxd4 6 ♗c4 ♕d6 7 0-0 ♘f6 8 ♘b3 ♘c6 9 ♘bxd4 ♘xd4 10 ♘xd4 a6 11 ♖e1 ♗d7 12 c3 ♕c7)

13   ♗b3

13   ...   ♗d6
13...0-0-0 14 ♕e2 ♗d6 15 h3 h6 16 a4 ♔b8 17 ♗e3 ♗h2+ 18 ♔h1 ♗f4 19 ♗xf4 ♕xf4 20 ♘f3 ♗c6 21 ♕e5+ ♕xe5 22 ♘xe5 ♖hf8 23 ♖ad1± (Breyther-Glek, Hamburg 1995).
14   h3   0-0-0
14...h6:
(a) 15 ♕f3 0-0-0 16 ♗e3 ♔b8 17 a4 e5 18 ♘c2 ♗c6 19 ♕e2 ♘d5= (Kosten-Speelman, British Ch 1991);
(b) 15 ♕e2!? 0-0-0 16 a4±.
15   ♕e2   ♔b8
16   a4   ♗c8
16...h6?! 17 ♗e3 ♖he8 18 ♘f3± (Adams-Speelman, British Ch 1991).

17	a5	♖hg8
18	♘f3	h6
19	♗e3	♘d7
20	♗a4	♗c5
21	b4	♗xe3
22	♕xe3	g5
23	b5	♕c5
24	♘d4±	

Adams-Akopian (Chalkidiki 1992).

19.232

(1 e4 e6 2 d4 d5 3 ♘d2 c5 4 exd5 ♕xd5 5 ♘gf3 cxd4 6 ♗c4 ♕d6 7 0-0 ♘f6 8 ♘b3 ♘c6 9 ♘bxd4 ♘xd4 10 ♘xd4 a6 11 ♖e1 ♗d7 12 c3 ♕c7)

13   ♕e2

13   ...   ♗d6
14   ♗g5
14 ♘f5?! ♗xh2+ 15 ♔h1 0-0 16 ♘xg7 ♔xg7 17 ♕e3 ♘g8 18 ♗d3 f5∓ (Coenen-Glek, Eupen 1993).
14   ...   0-0

15 g3

(a) 15 ♗xf6 gxf6 16 ♕g4+ ♔h8 17 ♕h4 ♖g8∞ (Canda-Vilela, Sagua la Grande 1989) – *Game 51*;

(b) 15 h3 ♗f4 16 ♗xf6 gxf6 17 ♗d3 ♔h8 18 ♕h5 f5 19 ♘xf5 exf5 20 ♖e7 ♕c6 21 ♖xd7 ♖g8 22 g4 ♕xd7 23 ♗xf5 ♗h2+± (Malishaus-kas-Luther, Groningen 1990).

15 ... ♖ae8
16 ♗d3±

Hjartarson-Nogueiras (Thessaloniki Olympiad 1988) – *Game 52*.

+--------------------------------+
| Game 44 |
| **Smagin–Akopian** |
| *Yerevan 1988* |
+--------------------------------+

1	e4	e6
2	d4	d5
3	♘d2	c5
4	♘gf3	cxd4
5	exd5	♕xd5
6	♗c4	♕d6
7	0-0	♘f6
8	♘b3	♘c6
9	♘bxd4	♘xd4
10	♘xd4	a6
11	♖e1	♕c7
12	♗d3	♗d6
13	♘f5?!	♗xh2+
14	♔h1	♔f8!

In this situation the best remedy against the knight thrust. 14...0-0? allows the familiar 15 ♘xg7! ♔xg7 16 ♕d2 with an attack, while the direct 14...h5?! 15 g3 h4 is parried by 16 ♗f4 ♕c6+ 17 ♔xh2 hxg3+ 18 ♔xg3 ♘h5+ 19 ♕xh5!±.

15 g3 exf5

16 ♔xh2 h5

17 ♗f4?

This plausible move loses quickly. The toughest defence was 17 ♖h1, aiming to neutralise the rook at h8, for example: 17...h4 18 ♔g1 ♔g8 (weaker is 18...h3 19 ♕f3 ♗e6?! 20 ♗xf5 ♗d5 21 ♕a3+ and 22 ♖xh3) 19 ♕f3 hxg3 20 ♖xh8+ ♔xh8 21 ♕xg3 with a reasonable position.

17 ... ♕b6
18 ♔g2 ♗e6
19 c4 h4
20 f3

Here 20 ♖h1 no longer saves White: 20...♘g4 21 ♕f3 ♗d7 or 21 ♕d2 ♖d8.

20 ... hxg3
21 ♗xg3 f4!
22 ♗f2

After 22 ♗xf4 Black wins by 22...♗h3+ 23 ♔g3 ♘h5+ 24 ♔xh3 ♘xf4+.

22 ... ♖h2+
White resigns

Game 45
Psakhis–Speelman
Moscow 1990

1	e4	e6
2	d4	d5
3	♘d2	c5
4	exd5	♕xd5
5	♘gf3	cxd4
6	♗c4	♕d6
7	0-0	♘f6
8	♘b3	♘c6
9	♘bxd4	♘xd4
10	♘xd4	a6
11	♖e1	♕c7
12	♗b3	♗d6
13	♘f5	

In this position the pawn sacrifice is considered justified.

13	...	♗xh2+
14	♔h1	♔f8

Recently Black has been experiencing difficulties after this move, and so 14...0-0 is more often played.

15 g3

The other main continuation 15 ♕d4 also does not promise Black an easy life.

| 15 | ... | ♗xg3 |

Black also has his problems after 15...exf5 16 ♗f4.

| 16 | ♘xg3 | b5 |

If 16...b6, apart from anything else White can play 17 ♕e2!? with the idea of ♕c4.

17 ♔g2!

Going to meet the bishop, but in the aims of self-defence (17...♗b7+ 18 f3). Less clear is 17 ♗e3 ♗b7+ 18 ♔g1 ♖d8.

| 17 | ... | h5 |

18 ♘f1?

Betraying the principle of aiming for a counter initiative, White comes under a strong attack. Speelman recommends the blockading 18 ♕d4! ♗b7+ (or 18...h4 19 ♗f4 ♕c6+ 20 ♘e4!) 19 f3 ♖d8 20 ♕h4! with advantage.

18	...	♗b7+
19	f3	h4
20	c3	h3+
21	♔h1	h2
22	♖e3	♘g4
23	♕e2	♘xe3
24	♗xe3	♖h3
25	♘d2	♖d8
26	♖f1?	

This loses quickly. 26 ♘e4 was a tougher defence.

26	...	♖xd2!
27	♗xd2	♖xf3
28	♕xf3	♗xf3+
29	♖xf3	♕c6

White resigns

Game 46
Geenen–Van Geldorp
Belgium 1990

1	e4	e6
2	d4	d5
3	♘d2	c5
4	exd5	♕xd5
5	♘gf3	cxd4
6	♗c4	♕d6
7	0-0	♘f6
8	♘b3	♘c6
9	♘bxd4	♘xd4
10	♘xd4	a6
11	♖e1	♕c7
12	♗b3	♗d6
13	♘f5	♗xh2+
14	♔h1	0-0
15	♘xg7	♔xg7

The main continuation is 15...♖d8.

16 ♕d4

White can also consider 16 ♕d2 ♘g8 17 ♕g5+ ♔h8 18 f4.

16 ... e5?!

With this move Black returns the piece, whereas 16...♗d6 17 ♗h6+ ♔g6 18 ♕h4 ♕c5 followed by ...h5 was possible.

17	♕h4	♘g4
18	f3	♕d8
19	♗g5!	f6
20	♗c1!	

20 fxg4 fxg5 21 ♕xh2 ♖f4 is less effective.

20	...	♗f4
21	♗xf4	♕d4
22	♗g3	♘e3
23	♕h2	♕xb2

If 23...♘f5 there would have followed 24 ♖xe5! But now the same idea proves decisive.

24	♖xe3!	♕xa1+
25	♖e1	♕b2
26	♖xe5	♗f5
27	♖e7+	♔h8
28	♕h6	♖g8
29	♗xg8	♖xg8
30	♗e5	♕b1+
31	♔h2	♖xg2+
32	♔xg2	♕xc2+
33	♔g3	

Black resigns

Game 47
Wolff–Gulko
USA Championship 1992

1	e4	e6
2	d4	d5
3	♘d2	c5
4	exd5	♕xd5
5	♘gf3	cxd4
6	♗c4	♕d6

7	0-0	♘f6
8	♘b3	♘c6
9	♘bxd4	♘xd4
10	♘xd4	a6
11	♗b3	♕c7
12	♖e1	♗d6
13	♘f5	♗xh2+
14	♔h1	0-0
15	♘xg7	♖d8
16	♕f3	♔xg7
17	g3	

17 ♗h6+ ♔g6 18 c3 is considered the main continuation.

17	...	b5
18	♔xh2	♗b7
19	♕f4	

Including the bishop by 19 ♗h6+? ♔g6 20 ♕f4 might lead to its loss after 20...♕c5.

19	...	♕c6

Black hopes to derive more from the exposed position of the white king than an equal ending after 19...♕xf4 20 ♗xf4 ♘g4+ 21 ♔g1 ♖ac8 22 ♗g5!

20	♖g1	♖d1!

21	♗e3	♖xa1
22	♕h6+	♔g8
23	♕g5+	♔f8
24	♕c5+	♔e8
25	♕xc6+	♗xc6
26	♖xa1	♘g4+

A real achievement from Black's manoeuvres — the creation of a weak pawn at e3.

27	♔h3	

After 27 ♔g1 ♘xe3 28 fxe3 ♖d8 the coordination of the rook with the bishop is more effective, for example: 29 ♖f1 a5! 30 a3 a4 31 ♗a2 ♗e4 32 c4 ♖d2 etc.

27	...	♘xe3
28	fxe3	♖d8
29	a4	b4
30	♗c4	a5
31	♗b5	♖c8
32	♗d3	♔e7
33	g4?!	

33 b3 was more prudent.

33	...	♖g8
34	♔h4	h6
35	♖f1	♖g5
36	b3	♖e5

36...f6! was more subtle, opening a way for the king to the kingside in the event of 37 ♖f4 ♖e5 38 e4 (or 38 ♖c4 ♗d5) 38...♔f7 39 ♔g3 ♔g6 40 ♔h3 ♔g5, when Black increases his advantage (Gulko).

37	♖e1	f6
38	♔g3	h5
39	gxh5	♖xh5
40	e4	♔d6
41	♔f4	♔c5
42	e5	f5
43	♗c4	♖h4+

44   ♔g5

44   ...   ♖xc4!

The decisive exchange sacrifice. Now White is unable to defend all his weaknesses.

45   bxc4   ♔xc4
46   ♖d1

Equally hopeless was the king manoeuvre 46 ♔f6 ♗d5 47 ♖f1 ♔c3 48 ♖f2 f4! 49 ♔e7 f3 50 ♔d6 b3, when Black wins (Gulko).

46	...	♗xa4
47	♖d6	♗xc2
48	♖xe6	♗a4!
49	♖a6	♔b5
50	♖a8	b3
51	e6	♔b4
52	♖b8+	♔a3
53	♔xf5	b2

White resigns

Game 48
Gufeld–Ravi
Calcutta 1994

1	e4	e6
2	d4	d5
3	♘d2	c5
4	exd5	♕xd5
5	♘gf3	cxd4
6	♗c4	♕d6
7	0-0	♘f6
8	♘b3	♘c6
9	♘bxd4	♘xd4
10	♘xd4	a6
11	♖e1	♕c7
12	♗b3	♗d6
13	♘f5	♗xh2+
14	♔h1	0-0
15	♘xg7	♖d8
16	♕f3	♔xg7
17	♗h6+	♔g6
18	c4?!	

A dubious idea. White prevents 18...♘d5, which is possible after the main continuation 18 c3, but another defensive resource for Black proves sufficiently effective.

18   ...   ♘h5!

Threatening by 19...♗f4 to curb the attack.

19   ♗e3

19 ♖e4 ♔xh6 20 ♖h4 is parried by 20...♕e5! 21 g4 ♔g7 22 ♖xh5 ♕xb2.

19   ...   f5
20   g4

Enforced activity, allowing the bishop at h2 to escape, since after 20 g3 b6 21 ♔xh2 ♗b7 the threats on the a8-h1 diagonal are too dangerous.

20	...	♘f6
21	gxf5+	exf5
22	♕g2+	♘g4!

23   f3   ♗d7

Now after 24 fxg4 ♗c6 25 gxf5+ ♚h5! the second bishop comes effectively into play.

24	♗c2	♗g3!
25	fxg4	♗c6
26	♗xf5+	♚g7
27	♗e4	♗xe1
28	♗h6+	♚xh6?

Tired by the preceding tense struggle, the Indian player is unable to withstand the second appearance of the bishop at h6, and the game ends in an amusing perpetual check to the black king, circling around the g4 pawn. Of course, he should have declined the Greek gift by retreating 28...♚g8.

29	♕h3+	♚g5
30	♕h5+	♚f4
31	♕f5+	♚g3
32	♕f3+	♚h4
33	♕f6+	♚g3
34	♕f3+	♚h4
35	♕f6+	♚g3

draw agreed

Game 49
Adams–Dreev
Wijk aan Zee 1996

1	e4	e6
2	d4	d5
3	♘d2	c5
4	exd5	♕xd5
5	♘gf3	cxd4
6	♗c4	♕d6
7	0-0	♘f6
8	♘b3	♘c6
9	♘bxd4	♘xd4
10	♘xd4	a6
11	♖e1	♕c7
12	♗b3	♗d6
13	♘f5	♗xh2+
14	♚h1	0-0
15	♘xg7	♖d8
16	♕f3	♚xg7
17	♗h6+	♚g6
18	c3	♘d5

In view of the debacle suffered by Black in the present game, his defences urgently need strengthening around here. 18...♘h5!? has

yet to be refuted: 19 ♗e3 (Gulko)
19...f5 20 g4 ♘f6, or 19 ♖e4 ♔xh6
20 ♖h4 ♕e5 (Khalifman), with an
unclear position in both cases.

19 ♖ad1!

Speelman's improvement over
the previous ideas of 19 ♖e4, 19 g3
and 19 ♗c1. For the moment White
does not force matters, but calmly
brings his last reserve into the
attack, the point being that his loose
bishop is still immune: 19...♔xh6
20 ♖xd5! ♖xd5 21 ♕f6+ ♔h5 22
♖e3 and wins.

The position is extremely difficult for Black to defend, since his
king is seriously exposed, and he
has great problems in bringing his
queenside pieces into play.

19 ...   f5

Adams gives 19...♗e5 (19...♗d6
20 ♗c1 f5 transposes to the game)
20 ♗c1 f5 (or 20...♔g7 21 ♕h5 f6
22 ♕h6+ ♔g8 23 f4 ♗d6 24 ♖xd5)
21 c4 ♘b4 22 ♖xd8 ♕xd8 23 ♖xe5
♘d3 24 ♕g3+ and wins, but in this
line 20...f6!? (Marin) may offer
more chances of resisting.

20 ♗c1   ♗d6

With 20...♗e5 21 c4 Black can
return the piece immediately:

(a) 21...♘b4 22 ♖xd8 ♕xd8 23
♖xe5 ♘d3 24 ♕g3+ ♔f7 25 ♗g5
♘xf2+ 26 ♔g1 ♕d4 27 ♗e3 ♘e4
28 ♕f4, and White's attack should
eventually prevail (Speelman);

(b) 21...♘f6 22 ♖xd8 ♕xd8 23
♖xe5 ♘g4 24 ♖e1 (if 24 ♕g3 ♕d3!
– Krantz) 24...♕h4+ 25 ♔g1 e5,
when the situation is totally unclear.

However, 21 g4!? (Krantz), de-
clining the piece but threatening to
open further lines for the attack,
leaves Black critically placed.

21 ♗xd5   exd5
22 ♖xd5   ♗d7

Or 22...♗e7 23 ♗f4 ♕c6 24
♖xe7 with a quick mate (Adams).

In *Mastering the French* Harley
and McDonald analyse the alternative defences 22...♖g8 and 22...
a5, but in each case the thematic 23
g4! fatally exposes the beleaguered
black king.

23 ♕h3   ♗f8
24 ♖e3

Once this rook reaches the g-file
it will be all over. 24...f4 does not
help, since then the other rook joins
the attack – 25 ♕h5+.

24 ...   ♔g7
25 ♖g3+   ♔h8
26 ♕h4   ♗e6
27 ♗f4   ♗e7
28 ♗xc7

Black lost on time, but in any
case he was about to be mated after
28...♗xh4 29 ♗e5+.

Game 50
Kotronias–Kramnik
Chalkidiki 1992

1	e4	e6
2	d4	d5
3	♘d2	c5
4	♘gf3	cxd4
5	exd5	♕xd5
6	♗c4	♕d6

7	0-0	♘f6
8	♘b3	♘c6
9	♘bxd4	♘xd4
10	♘xd4	a6
11	♗b3	♕c7
12	♖e1	♗d7
13	♗g5	0-0-0
14	c3	

After the common alternative 14 ♕f3 Black has the good manoeuvre 14...♗d6 15 h3 ♗h2+ 16 ♔h1 ♗e5.

14	...	♗d6
15	♗xf6	gxf6
16	♕h5	♖df8
17	g3	♕c5
18	♗d1	♖hg8!?

18...♕xh5 19 ♗xh5 ♔c7 20 ♖ad1 leads to an equal ending.

19 ♕xh7

White accepts the challenge, although Black's initiative is pretty strong.

19	...	f5
20	♗f3	♖h8
21	♕g7	f4

22 ♘b3?

Why drive the queen onto the attacking diagonal? After 22 ♖ad1 ♕c7 23 ♗g2 the white king's position is sufficiently solid.

22	...	♕c7
23	♖e2	

23 ♖ad1 would have allowed a similar attack: 23...fxg3 24 fxg3 ♖fg8 25 ♕xf7 ♗xg3 etc.

23	...	fxg3
24	fxg3	♖fg8!
25	♕f6	

It is dangerous to take the pawn: 25 ♕xf7 ♖f8 26 ♕g7 ♖hg8 27 ♕h7 ♗xg3! 28 hxg3 ♖xg3+! 29 ♗g2 ♖fg8 and Black wins (Kramnik).

25	...	♗xg3!
26	hxg3	♕xg3+
27	♖g2	♕h2+
28	♔f2	♖xg2+
29	♗xg2	♖g8
30	♖g1	♖g4!
31	♕e7	

If 31 ♔f3 Black wins by 31...e5! 32 ♕b6 ♖g3+ 33 ♔f2 ♗c6.

31	...	♖f4+
32	♔e2	♕xg1
33	♗xb7+	♔c7
34	♗f3	♕b6
35	♘c5	♕d6

36 ♕xd6+ ♔xd6 37 b4 ♗b5+ 38 ♔e3 ♖c4 39 ♘b7+ ♔c7 40 ♔d2 ♖f4 **White resigns**

Game 51
Canda–Vilela
Sagua la Grande 1989

1	e4	e6
2	d4	d5

3	♘d2	c5
4	♘gf3	cxd4
5	exd5	♕xd5
6	♗c4	♕d6
7	0-0	♘f6
8	♘b3	♘c6
9	♘bxd4	♘xd4
10	♘xd4	a6
11	♖e1	♗d7
12	c3	♕c7
13	♕e2	♗d6
14	♗g5	

Here the attack 14 ♘f5?! ♗xh2+ 15 ♔h1 0-0 16 ♘xg7 can be parried, since the bishop at c4 is not defended: 16...♔xg7 17 ♕e3 ♘g8!

14	...	0-0
15	♗xf6	

This move opens the g-file for Black.

15	...	gxf6
16	♕g4+	♔h8
17	♕h4	♖g8

Black loses immediately after 17...♕xc4? 18 ♕xf6+ ♔g8 19 ♖e4.

18	♕xf6+	♖g7
19	♖e4!	

19	...	♖ag8?!

19...♔g8! was essential.

20	♘f3?!	

After 20 ♗d3!, in view of the threat of ♖h4 White would have forced the exchange of queens, remaining a pawn up. But now too this threat is still present (20...♗c6? 21 ♖h4! ♗e7 22 ♖xh7+! ♔xh7 23 ♗d3+).

20	...	♕c5!
21	♗f1	

Now against 21 ♖h4 Black had prepared a defence: 21...♗e7 22 ♖xh7+ ♔xh7 23 ♗d3+ ♖g6 24 ♕xf7+ ♔h6 25 ♗xg6 ♖xg6 (Vilela).

21	...	♗e7
22	♕e5	♗c6!
23	♖e3	♕xe5
24	♘xe5	♗xg2
25	♘xf7+?	

An oversight. After 25 ♖g3! ♗xf1 26 ♔xf1 the game is level.

25	...	♖xf7
26	♗xg2	♗c5!
27	♖d3	♖xf2
28	♖g3	♖f6+!

White resigns

Game 52
Hjartarson–Nogueiras
Thessaloniki Olympiad 1988

1	e4	e6
2	d4	d5
3	♘d2	c5
4	exd5	♕xd5
5	♘gf3	cxd4
6	♗c4	♕d6

7	0-0	♘f6
8	♘b3	♘c6
9	♘bxd4	♘xd4
10	♘xd4	a6
11	♖e1	♗d7
12	c3	♕c7
13	♕e2	♗d6
14	♗g5	0-0
15	g3	♖ae8
16	♗d3	

Black was prepared for 16 ♖ad1 ♘d5!?, not fearing the isolated pawn after 17 ♗xd5 exd5 18 ♕f3 ♕a5! 19 a3 ♖e4, with equal chances.

16	...	♘d5

Of course, not 16...e5? 17 ♗xf6 exd4 18 ♗xh7+!

17	♖ad1	♗e7
18	h4	

18 ♗c1 is also possible, with the idea of 18...♗f6 19 ♕e4.

18	...	♗c5!
19	♗c2	f5
20	♕f3	h6
21	♗c1	♘f6
22	♗b3	♗xd4

23	♖xd4?	

This allows Black to advance his e-pawn and to activate his pieces in the direction of the kingside. 23 cxd4 was better.

23	...	♔h8!
24	♖ed1	♗c6
25	♕e2	e5
26	♖d6	f4
27	♗c2	♕c8!
28	♗g6	♖e7

Also possible was 28...♕h3 29 ♖xc6 bxc6 30 ♗xe8 ♖xe8 with a strong attack.

29	b3	

Relying on his outpost bishop at g6, White agrees to a position that is inferior, even though he wins the exchange. But perhaps he should have sacrificed the exchange? For example: 29 gxf4 ♕h3 30 ♖xc6 bxc6 31 ♖d3 ♕xh4 32 ♖g3 etc.

29	...	♕h3
30	f3	♕xg3+
31	♕g2	♕xf3
32	♕xf3	♗xf3
33	♖d8	♖ee8!
34	♖xe8	♖xe8

Now 35 ♖f1 ♗e2 36 ♖e1 f3 37 ♗xe8 ♘xe8 would have won the exchange, and although it would not have been easy to activate the rook, White should have been consistent.

35	♖d6?	♖c8
36	c4	♗c6
37	♗b2	f3!
38	♗xe5	f2+
39	♔f1	♘g4
40	♗f4	♖f8
41	♖d4	♘e5!

42	h5	♘f3
43	♖d1	♔g8
44	♗g3	♘d2+
45	♖xd2	♗g2+
46	♔xg2	f1=♕+

47	♔h2	♕c1
48	♖d7	♕e3
49	♖c7	♖f2+!
50	♔h3	♕e6+

White resigns

List of Illustrative Games

Index of Variations